DATE DUE

JUL 0 5 2009	
APR 2 1 2010	
MAR 0 7 2011	
APR 2 6 2012	
MAY 0 8 2012	

BRODART, CO. Cat. No. 23-221-003

THE
ENCYCLOPEDIA OF
MOSAIC TECHNIQUES

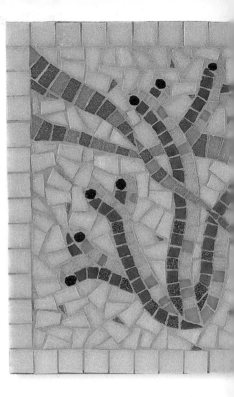

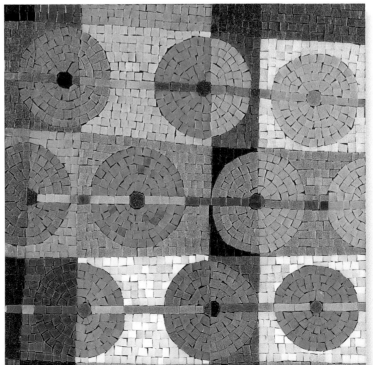

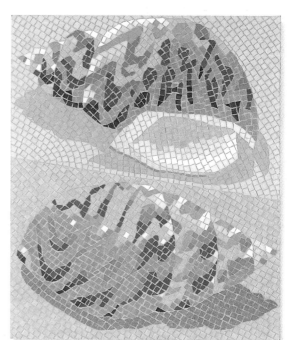

THE
ENCYCLOPEDIA OF
MOSAIC TECHNIQUES

Emma Biggs

RUNNING PRESS
PHILADELPHIA · LONDON

9 8 7

Digit on the right indicates the number of this printing.

Library of Congress Cataloging-in-Publication Number 98-68227

ISBN 0-7624-0444-2

This book was designed by:
Quarto Publishing plc
The Old Brewery
6 Blundell Street
London N7 9BH

Senior editor Anna Watson
Copy editors Stephanie Driver, Claire Waite
Art editor Sally Bond
Designer Paul Wood
Photographer Martin Norris, Les Weis
Illustrator Dave Kemp
Picture researcher Gill Metcalfe
Assistant art director Penny Cobb
Art director Moira Clinch
Publisher Marion Hasson

Manufactured in Singapore by United Graphics (Pte) Ltd.

Printed in Singapore by Star Standard Industries (Pte) Ltd.

This book may be ordered by mail from the publisher.

Please include $2.50 for postage and handling.

But try your bookstore first!

Running Press Book Publishers
125 South Twenty-second Street
Philadelphia, Pennsylvania 19103-4399

Visit us on the web!
www.runningpress.com

Safety Notice

Mosaic-making can be dangerous, and readers should follow safety procedures and wear protective clothing and goggles at all times during the preparation of tiles and the making and fitting of mosaics. Neither the author, copyright holders, nor publishers of this book can accept legal liability for any damage or injury sustained as a result of making mosaics.

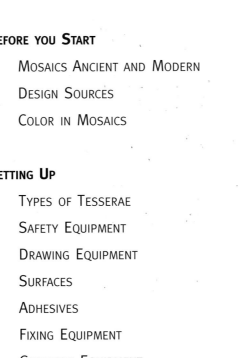

Contents

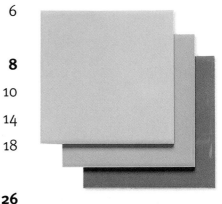

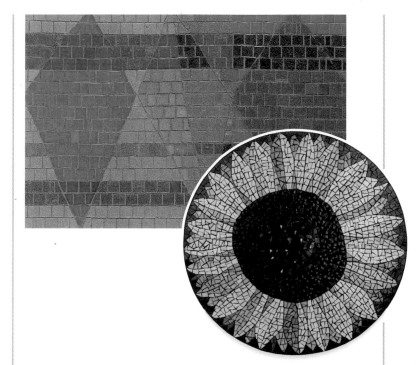

Introduction

All the essential techniques you need to make striking and unique mosaics are in this book, from cutting and laying tiles to creating your own intricate designs.

The book is a detailed and thorough technical guide to working in mosaic, starting with a brief history. It describes the characteristics of a wide range of different materials and why you might wish to use one rather than another. It sets out the stages of designing a mosaic, reveals the possible problems you might encounter, and gives you tips about how to avoid them. It clearly details what you will need to make a mosaic, where to look for inspiration for your designs, and how to use color creatively. It gives you practical and professional advice about choosing which grout to use, and makes clear which adhesive is the appropriate choice for any location.

All these issues are covered in the first section of the book. This is followed by an A to Z of Mosaic Techniques which runs through all the various mosaic techniques, giving detailed information about how to cut tiles and lay tesserae, through to grouting and fixing. The techniques are listed alphabetically to make it easy to use. The photographs of completed mosaics which follow in the Gallery section aim to stimulate you into thinking of new ways to work in the medium. They provide a range of designs you could use, but should also inspire you to create your own. Finally there is a glossary which explains any technical terminology.

Each technique is set out in as clear a manner as possible. Firstly, an introduction explains what circumstances make one preferable to another, then there is a list explaining what tools and materials are needed. Each technique is described carefully in a series of steps, and each step is accompanied by a photograph. This should make the process pretty foolproof. There is a photograph of each finished project, and cross-referencing throughout.

I wrote this book because I remember what it was like when I became interested in mosaic. The techniques seemed baffling and sound practical advice was difficult to come by. I have tried to give answers to the kinds of questions I think I would have asked, in as clear a way as possible. Mosaic is endlessly stimulating and fascinating. The more you do, the richer it seems. Whether you plan to make a career of it, or simply to make something thoroughly individual for your home, I hope that this book will help and encourage you, and also give you some of the enjoyment I have gained from working in this medium.

▲ There are many different ways of laying tiles in a mosaic. See laying tesserae (pages 98–101).

◀ This broken-crockery tabletop is suitable for use outside and was made using the outdoor direct adhesive method (see pages 112–113).

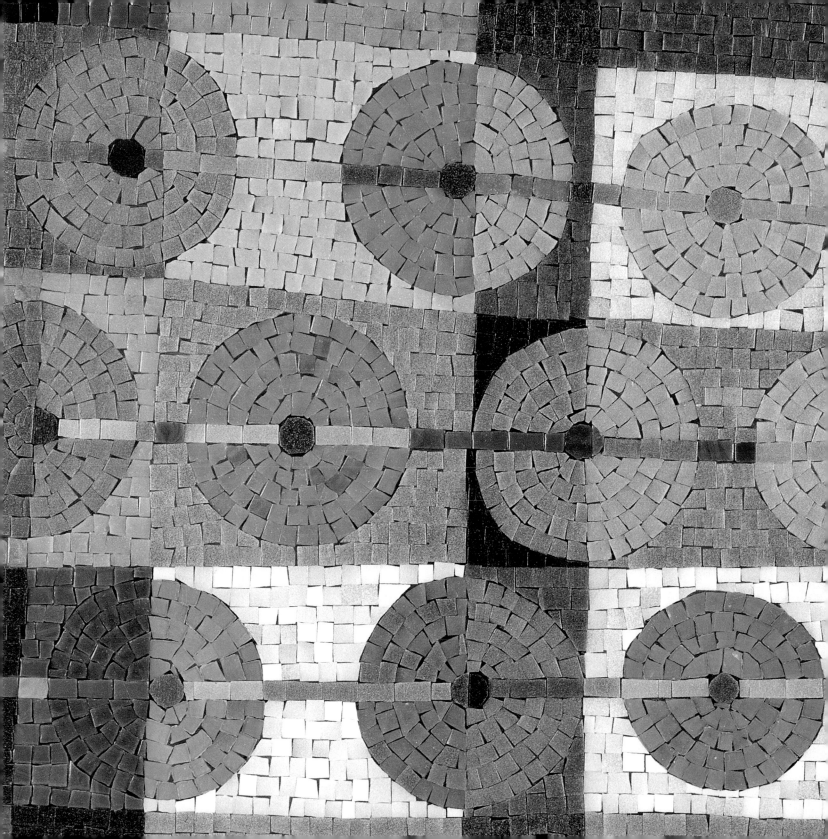

BEFORE YOU START

Mosaics Ancient and Modern

The history of mosaic seems to begin in the ancient Near East, with some of the earliest-known pieces, made with pebbles of contrasting colors, coming from Greece. It was the Romans, however, who really developed the art of mosaic.

Roman mosaic was often made from local stones, although glass was sometimes combined with natural materials to give highlights of color. It was commonly used as a flooring material and was also fairly widely used on walls. The ravages of time, however, have meant that less mural work still exists.

The finest, most intricate mosaic was made in small panels, of which many have survived from Pompeii, the Roman city that was buried by the volcanic eruption of Vesuvius. One of these is the truly fabulous and justly famous portrait of a Campanian lady. She might well have been the owner of the house of Julia Felix, a rich and respected woman who fell on hard times. The portrait is known as a micromosaic because the tiles are extremely small. It has such liveliness that makes you feel you could recognize her walking down the street. Highly-crafted decorative panels like these are known as "emblema," and Suetonius, the Roman biographer, tells us that Caesar took them on campaigns with him to decorate the floor of his tent.

Mosaic was not only produced in a highly-sophisticated manner. You can also see it in more ordinary domestic settings. The Roman "Beware of the Dog" house entrance mosaic floors were the equivalent of our decorative doormats. Even the pavements of Pompeii were decorated with simple stone and marble patterns. The marble, however, does not seem to have been local to Naples, which suggests that trading was lucrative, making the importation of marble economically possible.

In the early Christian period an enormous amount of highly-sophisticated glass smalti work was produced. The mosaics in Ravenna, Italy, are rightly some of the most well-known. One is a portrait of the Empress Theodora, whose father was a bear-keeper and mother an acrobat. She was an actress and courtesan, and Procopius, the Byzantine historian, tells extremely saucy stories about her. In spite of, or perhaps because of her sexual antics, she ended up marrying the Emperor Justinian. You would never be able to guess her racy nature from her mosaic portrait—she looks rather proud and imperious.

Mosaic was very popular as church decoration. The Norman mosaics at the cathedral in Monreale, Sicily, are like a fabulous comic strip depicting the Bible. You can see Abraham on the point of sacrificing poor Isaac, and Noah's family all peering out of portholes in the Ark. These lively scenes are inspiring for their color, form, and treatment, and their narrative content encompasses everything from the Creation to the Feeding of the

Five Thousand. There are many religious mosaics to be seen in Europe and whether it is the severed, worm-eaten heads of the damned from the church at Torcello in Italy, or the sweet scenes of Noah encouraging the birds into the ark from St. Mark's Cathedral in Venice, they are all worth studying both for their content and their beauty.

After the Renaissance the art of mosaic went into a decline. It became a copyists medium, making breathtaking, technically impressive copies of paintings, which rather make you wonder why they didn't paint them in the first place.

There was a revival of interest in the mid-19th century. As European countries acquired land and imperial ambitions, they looked back to the arts and architecture of the classical world for inspiration. There was a fashion for the antique, and a fashion for mosaic came with it. When the British built their civic buildings, with money gained from their new empire, they looked back to how the Romans had done it. Many Victorian civic buildings are direct copies of ones from the classical world, and they contain a lot of mosaic. This interest in an earlier empire was Europe-wide, and in a microcosmic way had dramatic consequences for one area of Italy.

The Italians have always divided mosaic into three categories. Marble and stone work is known as Roman mosaic. Fine mural work using smalti and vitreous glass is called Venetian mosaic.

▲ EMPRESS THEODORA
This detail from a 6th-century mosaic in Ravenna shows the typical Byzantine style of setting figures against a dazzling gold background.

▲ MOSAIC IN POMPEII
Despite suffering damage during the volcanic erruption that buried Pompeii, the subtle tones and intricate detailing of this mosaic from the 1st century BC have survived sufficiently well to amaze us over 2000 years later.

▶ BEWARE OF THE DOG
This domestic mosaic from Pompeii shows how prevalent mosaic was in Roman times. It is now on show in the National Archeological Museum, Naples.

Florentine mosaic is made with semi-precious stones and the individual pieces are so tightly jointed they have to be ground into place. Both Roman and Venetian mosaic became popular all over Europe during the 19th century. The skilled Roman mosaic workers all came from one area of Italy, Friuli, a region north of Venice. Work like this in marble and stone was labor-intensive and had traditionally been done on site. The craftsmen were used to moving around rather than working from the studio like the Venetian mosaic workers. Suddenly their skills were in great demand. Friulani craftsmen set up companies all over Europe. The demand for skilled workers was so great that a mosaic school was set up in one of the villages to train them. It still survives as an internationally renowned school of mosaic. In some of the villages, like Fanna, every available young man capable of mosaic work was taken and employed in the trade. If you walk round the cemetery of the little Friuli village of Sequals you will see the beautiful mosaic gravestones of generations of mosaic workers. Look up "mosaic" in the telephone directory today and you will find the same names.

There is still controversy raging in the mosaic world as to who invented the reverse method. Some people believe it was invented centuries ago, and that the Romans used it, others firmly adhere to the view that it was invented in the 19th century by the Venetian firm Salviati. Whatever the truth, the Venetian firm certainly popularized the method which most mosaic companies use today. Venice is still an essential spot on the mosaic map. The big Salviati factory (near the Guggenheim Museum) is now closed down, but Orsoni, the family firm who make smalti mosaic, is still there. There was a rumor that they were leaving Venice, but when I asked Lucio Orsoni about this he said "look around you, if you were me, would you move?"

The Italian-owned mosaic companies executed almost all the significant mosaic commissions, including Boris Anrep's work for Westminster Cathedral. Anrep was a Russian émigré, and a painter. He found Byzantine mosaic inspiring and his gift in using flickery descriptive color really lends itself to mosaic treatment. His floors for London's National Gallery are full of character and incident, and range in subject matter from a portrait of Winston Churchill to a Christmas pudding.

The Mexican muralists had laudable social ambitions for their work. Their socialist realist mosaics extol working-class virtues with literal narrative content, rather like community art. Mosaic played much the same role in the Soviet Union. The underground system in Moscow features scenes from the Revolution and mosaic was widely used as a visual aid to advertise socialist values.

The work of Antoni Gaudí is often described as fun, although it had serious aims. In fact most of the mosaic work that is celebrated as Gaudí's is by his collaborator, the

► BYZANTINE MOSAIC
These lambs are a detail from the incredible mosaics which cover the interior of the Basilica of St. Apollinare in Classe, Ravenna. They date from about 536 to 550 AD.

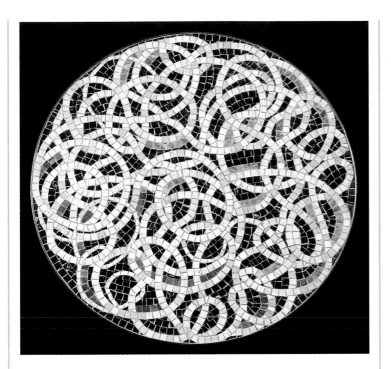

▲ ABSTRACT PATTERNS
Contemporary mosaic-makers have a tremendous range of art historical sources to draw upon. Some are inspired by Byzantine figurative work; others by the geometry of interlocking Roman borders. This piece is highly modernistic and uses the simple idea of following a random line to create a striking abstract motif.

experienced ceramicist Josep Maria Jujol. In Barcelona's Parque Güell you can see vast architectural-scale collages of waste material from ceramic factories. It is not clear whether Gaudí ever actually made any mosaic, but Jujol certainly did, and the decisions about color, pattern, and design seem to have been all his. He organized teams of workers to produce the mosaics, and corrected their work where he felt it was needed.

Mosaic is still utilized today. Venice is full of fabulous mosaic from churches to coffee bars, but it also has the distinctive tradition of mosaic advertisements set into the splendid ancient paving. Modern mosaic advertisements for local nightspots vie with vitreous glass promotions for a tourist essential, Kodak's newest films. Its hard to imagine another city encouraging it, but it would be good if they did. There is also a renewed interest in the craft and its modern-day decorative appeal in the home and garden. I hope that this history has inspired you to experiment with this ancient craft and that this whole book gives you the back up and the confidence you need to become an accomplished mosaicist yourself.

▶ GAUDI AND JUJOL
Spanish architect Antoni Gaudí used Josep Maria Jujol's ceramic mosaics to complement his organic shapes, as on this bench at a viewpoint in the Parque Güell, Barcelona.

Design Sources

Once you have started to work in mosaic, you will begin to notice mosaic-like qualities in all sorts of ordinary objects around you. When you are looking for visual images to inspire you, a useful starting point might be anything you have collected because it appealed to you.

This might be anything from postcards to pebbles from a beach. Try to work out why you are attracted to these objects—because of their color, design, shape, or texture? Once you know why something appeals to you, it will be easier to produce a working design from it. For instance, if the pebbles appeal to you because of their soft, natural colors, then consider making a mosaic from pebbles or from similar colors of riven marble. If the postcards appeal to you because of their bright colors or simplified designs, you could work on a panel for your kitchen or bathroom which uses bright sea-and-sand colors or recreates a beach scene.

The most compelling creative impulses come from something which stimulates you, and which makes you feel driven to investigate further. Don't pursue something just because you feel it ought to be interesting to you. If it doesn't genuinely excite you as a theme or as subject matter, that lack of interest may well come across in how you work, and the piece will be less appealing as a result.

☞
Color in mosaics,
pages 18–25
Tesserae, pages 28–33
Design techniques,
pages 70–73

THE NATURAL WORLD

No matter how many times a subject has been looked at, if it genuinely interests you, you will have something new to bring to it. Subjects don't get exhausted by being looked at again and again, they often become richer and more interesting. You start to see things in them that you previously missed, or having dealt with the subject in mosaic, you start to see the thing itself in a new way. Fish are a popular subject in mosaic, probably because of their scales, which suit interpretation in mosaic. Birds are another recurring theme, as their feathers can be treated in a very naturalistic way by mosaic tiles.

▼ Tropical fish are particularly inspiring for mosaicists, as their bright colors and intricate patterns can be recreated in bright shades of tiles.

► The colors of a hummingbird are beautiful, but the subject might seem too intricate for mosaic. Don't be discouraged, though. You could either work in micromosaic (see page 102) for a realistic effect, or you could simplify the shapes and work in normal size tiles.

◄ The delicate leaf shapes and rich fall colors of this Japanese maple could be translated into a beautiful panel for a garden, giving color all year round.

TEXTILES

Textiles are a rich source of inspiration, and a relationship between mosaic and woven fabrics is not new: for example, ancient examples of Coptic weaving show the influence of traditional mosaic patterns in carpet borders. There is a clear link between stitches and tesserae. Repeated patterns are also common to both mosaic and textiles.

▲ This kilim uses close tones and color contrast in a subtle and interesting way. Perhaps you have a favorite rug, or some textile you have chosen specifically for its color. You may be able to make a mosaic in similar colors. The more you think about color and experiment with it, the more your color sense will develop.

▼ The pretty bell-shaped flowers of Campanula could be translated into a lovely border pattern. Careful cutting of tiles to capture the shapes of the petals would be necessary, but the fresh contrast of pale purple flowers against a dark green background would really look stunning if made up in vitreous glass tiles.

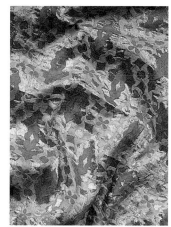

◄ The charm of this fabulous sari relies on surface reflection: when the gold weave isn't catching the light it is close in tone to the peach fabric. When light catches parts of the gold design as the sari-wearer moves, the patterns is sometimes vibrant or seems to vanish. In mosaics you could use gold or silver pieces to give a similar glimmering effect.

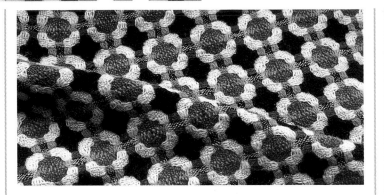

▲ There are very few really good pinks produced in glass mosaic. Perhaps that novelty is part of what makes this fabric so appealing. It benefits from the richness and complexity of a simple repeat pattern, and the way new shades are created from mixing two colors. It is also fascinating to see the way the pattern is broken by the fold in the cloth. Drapery, folds, and the way patterns break are always of interest to mosaicists.

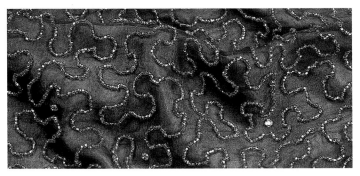

▲ The use of these tiny beads has a mosaic-like quality. Subtle differences between the decorative work, made lively through being reflective, and its close-toned background, have lessons for the mosaicist.

▲ This bold, simple fabric, with contrasting sizes of effects and bright, slightly off colors, shows that simplicity is not boring. Size contrasts can be very striking. The bright colors appear more lively against a black and white field.

▼ These delicate colors provide a lesson in subtlety—it is not necessary to use loud colors to create an impact. Although close tones are difficult to use, when they work, as they do here, they can be very pleasing.

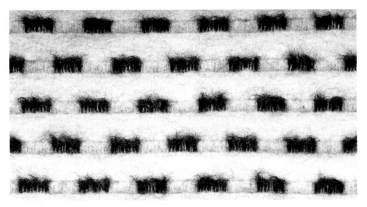

◀ This blanket shows texture, contrast, and repetition, all of which are relevant to the mosaicist. The design might be simple but the effect is dramatic.

ABSTACT IDEAS

You may find, though, that the thing which really drives you is not a particular subject matter, but the mosaic-making process itself. There is an immense amount of interest to be derived from simply investigating what the medium enables you to do. Allow yourself to be led by the colors or textures of the tiles. Play with the different effects created by reflective and matte surfaces, or with cutting contrasts. Search out unusual objects or abstract images which you can turn into patterns or color themes for a mosaic panel or border.

◀ This mirrored bathroom, by Fran Soler, is completely abstract but endlessly fascinating. Most of the wall surfaces are covered with randomly cut pieces of mirror, but some larger areas of plain mirror have been included to serve a practical purpose.

▼ This tabletop by Norma Vondee uses the subtle tones of blue-and-white crockery to give subtle variations within a simple abstract pattern.

▲ Geometric patterns, such as this one based on interlocking circles, require careful planning, but also give very effective results when made into a two-color mosaic.

▲ Noticing the pattern of bubbles rising through water could inspire your color use in a mosaic, but also consider cutting shapes. A few circular tesserae set within a fairly plain Opus Regulatum background would capture the impression of bubbles.

CONCLUSION

You will find that mosaic itself can provide a rich source of inspiration for you when designing a new mosaic. The Gallery of mosaics at the end of this book (pages 132–155) is an ideal starting point. You can also try looking through art and architectural books at your local library, subscribing to craft magazines, or visiting your nearest museum. Finally, be alert to the many mosaics —old and new—which may decorate shops, offices, and public buildings in your area.

Color in Mosaics

Design, composition, technical competence and cutting ability are all important aspects of mosaic making, but one of the most fundamental skills involved in creating a successful mosaic is the use of color.

Some people seem to have more of an interest in and an aptitude for color than others. However, through observation, it is possible to learn how to use color to great effect.

Mosaic is unusual among creative mediums in that it does not really allow for color mixing. The mosaic palette is fixed by the color of the material and you will need to design your work with this fixed range of colors in mind. Although distance allows for some fusion of colors, you are unlikely to benefit from this effect with most domestic projects.

One consequence of having a fixed palette is the need for stylization. If something is either one color or another there is not much scope for indecision, or the hazy transition from one area of color to another that painting allows. The results of working within these constraints can be pleasingly bold, but they can also result in designs that are far from subtle in effect.

ADAPTING COLOR FOR MOSAIC A good example of how this might work is to think about water and how it is commonly represented by the hue of blue or turquoise-green—as it happens, owing to the fact that a great deal of mosaic is used for swimming pools, the range of blues and greens is fairly

☞
**Design sources,
pages 14–18
Drawing equipment,
pages 36–37
Gallery, pages 132–155**

Design sources, pages 14–18; Drawing equipment, pages 36–37; Gallery, pages 132–155

▼ **COLOR WHEEL**
This shows the traditional way of considering colors. The primary colors are red, yellow and blue, and the secondary colors are purple, green and orange. In mosaic you can create an impression of a color, such as orange from red and yellow, by inter-mixing tiles but the optical effect only works from a distance.

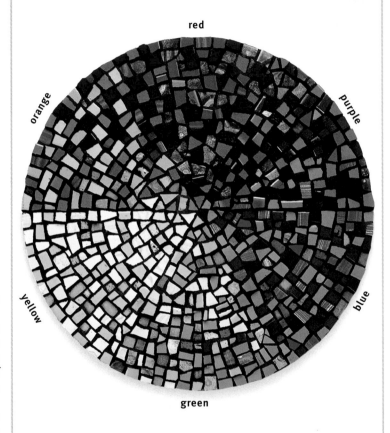

red

orange

purple

yellow

blue

green

extensive. However, it is not often that we see bodies of intense blue or green water inland—these are reserved for the idyllic shores of the Mediterranean or the Caribbean. Instead, water inland often actually looks black. Therefore, we associate water with blue when, in actual fact, another color would look more realistic used in a mosaic scene. So, for example, where you might wish to use yellow, you may well find that a buff or beige-brown does just as well, if not better.

Fundamentally, you will find that the use of color in mosaic is not always straightforward, and in order to make the most of the range of effects mosaic can allow, you really need to understand hue, tone, and intensity.

◄ THE MOSAIC PALETTE
The colors that you can obtain in vitreous glass (left) and smalti (top left) range from somber to very bright. Extra interest can be gained by using gold or silver (top center) or gold-veined vitreous glass tiles (above center). The palette of colors is rather restricted, so it is important to consider the color relationships within your mosaic. Colors can be classed as either warm or cool (above right) and a warm-colored motif will stand out effectively against a background of cool colors. Using only warm or cool colors in a piece will give it a strongly atmospheric effect.

HUE When we use the word color we are actually talking about hue: the place that color has in the spectrum. Blue is one hue, yellow is another.

Some mosaic materials offer a wider range of hues than others. In the eighteenth century the Vatican workshops produced literally thousands of different colors, with so wide a range that it was possible for mosaicists to make precise copies of paintings. Today the range is much smaller, and there are some hues which have ranges that are decidedly limited. Yellow is a color which is rather inadequately represented, for example. There are one or two mauves, but there is no true purple. The range of pinks extends to about two. With such limitations you have to rely on using context rather than color to make sense of your mosaic.

TONE The tone of a color is a description of how light or dark it is, therefore a blue and a green may be the same tone, even though they are different hues. For the purposes of most work in mosaic there are really only three main tonal divisions. These are dark, mid-tone, and light. You will notice, particularly when a mosaic is grouted, that similar tones have more in common with one another than similar hues, or similar degrees of intensity. This can have both a beneficial and a problematic consequence. The use of close tones can create remarkably subtle effects, but at the risk of losing the clarity of an image.

SIMILAR TONES
▲ This mosaic uses a relationship of closely toned hues, but this time the degree of lightness is equal, giving a harmonious effect.

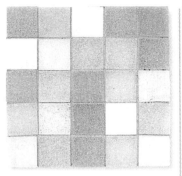

SIMILAR INTENSITIES
▲ The white tiles are much brighter than the other tiles in this piece, but in this case they make the mosaic look fresh and lively. Although the white tiles contrast with their mid-tone to light background, the tonal relationship between them is close. Here, intensity is used to enhance and emphasize the color relationships.

COMPLIMENTARY TONES
▲ Although the hues in this mosaic are distinctly different, the tiles fuse together because they are close in tone: they carry the same degree of darkness.

VARYING INTENSITIES
▲ The yellow in this piece illustrates a distinct difference in intensity of color. The yellow is much brighter than the other colors and stands out dramatically. In a large mosaic you would have to balance the amount of intense color across the whole mosaic.

INTENSITY Intensity is a word used to describe the weight of a color. This may be its relative brightness or lack of it, but chiefly refers to the strength the color has.

For example, there is a very dense and intense brown in vitreous glass mosaic. The intensity of this color outweighs that of any equivalent and makes it tremendously difficult to use. Perhaps by using another intensely bright color it would be possible to balance the intense weight of the brown, but it is a characteristic particular to this color that it manages to be intense without actually being bright. It weighs more heavily than the colors around it, and can easily throw a composition out of balance.

Although use of color is surrounded by a series of conventions, the best lesson you can learn is to be constantly experimenting and making comparisons yourself. It is remarkable how easily we carry around rules and assumptions with us which we believe, but have never really examined. Through observation and comparison you can develop your color insight to the point where some combinations seem to give visceral pleasure, and others simply seem flat. A sense of color is like a sense of taste: the more you develop it, the richer and more varied is the pleasure it can give you.

CONTRASTING HUES
▲ The yellow pieces in this mosaic contrast with the blue background tiles in both hue and intensity, but a visual link is made because of the gold veining running through the vitreous blue glass.

COMPLIMENTARY HUES
▲ If you have a plain background area to fill, you can avoid boring areas of flat color by mixing different hues, such as the red and brown here, provided that you keep the tones close.

COLORED GROUT The effect grout has on the relationship between colors within the mosaic cannot be over-emphasized. Grout unites the surface of a mosaic, thus creating a connection between the colored tiles, with varying consequences. With this in mind it is clear to see that grout should not be an afterthought, but an absolutely fundamental consideration when you are designing a mosaic. Obviously it takes a certain amount of experience to be able to foresee how the grout you use is going to affect the finished appearance of a mosaic, but there are certain basic principles that you can bear in mind in order to help you plan your design and your choice of colors.

Grout can either be used to draw the image together, giving the mosaic a greater sense of unity and completeness, or it can be used to fracture a piece to give a busy and lively effect. Whichever option you choose for a particular piece, the color balance you see while you are making the mosaic will change dramatically once the piece has been grouted. To keep the

◀ This panel has been grouted using white grout. This has a very fracturing effect on bright colors which are not light in tone. It has recently been a fashionable grout, however, probably because we associate white with cleanliness and freshness. Its cultural associations make it popular even when its tonal relationship to the mosaic wouldn't necessarily seem to make it a logical choice.

VITREOUS GLASS
▲ This sample is ungrouted mosaic. Note the luminescence with which the colors relate to one another. People often think of mosaic as being like pointillist painting. In fact it is only where the colors have a chance to relate to one another without the intervening medium of grout, as here, that there is much of a similarity. Once the piece has been grouted, as illustrated in the following three samples, the uniform joint color prevents the colors of the tiles relating directly to one another, and the intense luminosity is muted or lost.

balance as close to the original as possible, a good general rule is to grout the mosaic in the predominant tone of the piece.

There are three main tonal options for grout. These are white, mid-gray, and dark gray (some manufacturers do produce a black). If the main tone is predominantly dark or bright, choose the darkest grout. If the main tone is in the mid-range, choose mid-gray. For the lightest, palest tones, choose white. Although inevitably you will have some areas which vary from the predominant tone, by observing these general rules you will keep the balance as even as possible.

The following small panels are useful aides when you are trying to decide which grout color to choose. Do consult them, or better still, make your own.

◄ Here the same vitreous glass sample is grouted in gray. This makes the glass seem soft and subtle. Of all the samples, this seems most to bring out the illusion of depth: some colors seem to recede, others to come closer.

◄ Here you can see the effect of dark grout. The color balance is probably closest to the ungrouted piece. You can observe color depth, and color brightness is highlighted sharply too. Look at the way the gray and the dark grout unite the mid- and dark tones in different ways.

CERAMIC
▲ Here a ceramic mosaic panel has been grouted with white grout. It illustrates the way the white grout draws attention to the paler colors of the piece.

◄ When grouted with gray, the same mosaic panel looks quite different. The mid-toned grout brings out the mid-toned ceramic tiles. The range of colors in ceramic is fairly limited. If you are working in black and white, gray grout is usually the most sensible choice since it fractures both tones equally, rather than giving tonal precedence to one over the other. Many of the middle range of ceramic colors are similar in tone to the grout. This can, however, have the unfortunate effect of drawing mid-tones together and making strange united patches in what otherwise would be an evenly fractured mosaic. To overcome this problem, add a little lighter or a little darker grout to the gray mix, making a note of the proportions you mix.

▲ In this example the ceramic mosaic panel has been grouted with dark grout, again producing a different effect. Here, the darkest tones in the tiles are accentuated by the dark grout.

Ceramic tiles can stain, so it is not advisable to leave dark grout smeared across them for any length of time.

◄ Gray grout seems to give a softness to the material and emphasizes the subtleties of the marbled surface.

MARBLE
▼ The white grout in this marble mosaic panel brings out the intensity of the colors in the tiles. It fractures the piece and gives emphasis to the lines of coursing.

▲ Dark grout stresses a different set of tonal relationships to those you notice when the mosaic has been grouted in gray or white. Uniting the dark tones of the marble tiles intensifies the colors and creates an illusion of the lightest advancing and darkest tiles receding.

ANALYZING COLOR These projects from the A to Z of Techniques have been chosen here to illustrate some key issues of using tile and grout color in mosaics. The key to success in mosaic-making lies in experimentation and practice—even experienced mosaicists will make errors of judgment in their color use. The important thing is not to be disheartened and, if you are unsatisfied with one piece, resolve to make the next one better.

▶ The background to this starfish panel has been grouted using a color which draws it together. It allows the starfish to be read as a clear image against a flickery background. The grout color has helped to give clarity to the piece.

▲ This bowl demonstrates the way in which a piece can be made lively with only small spots of bright color. Although there is some tonal variation in the blues and greens, it is the orange tiles that are most eye-catching. Be moderate in your use of bright colors since they appear to be more intense if their use is limited.

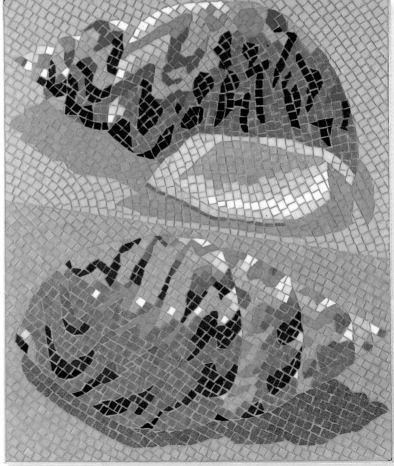

▶ This panel depicting two shells demonstrates the fracturing nature of grout color. Although the gray grout works well for the background, it is too light in tone for the shells. These would be less lost against the field if they had been grouted using a darker color. The problem arises because tiles of a similar color and tone have been used both in the background and in the shells. If the darker shell color were united by a darker grout the piece would have greater clarity.

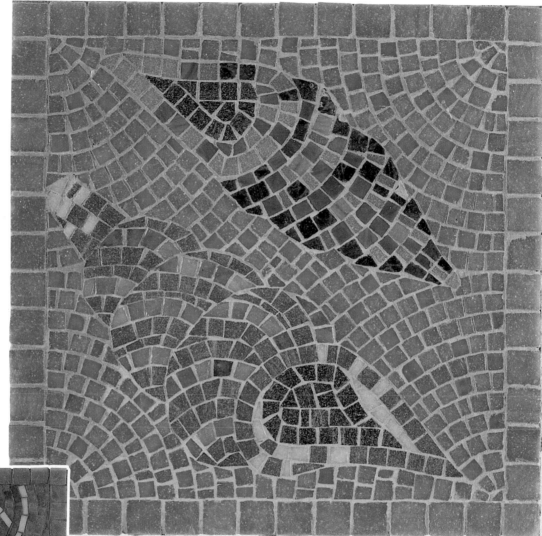

▼ The fish panel demonstrates how color can balance form. The shape and density of the fish is compositionally balanced by the bright color of the weed. This is a useful lesson for when you are designing a mosaic. It is not necessary for color to be balanced by color. Likewise there is no need for perfect symmetry.

▲ Here we can see tonal color and the way it affects form. Using a darker tone of one color gives the impression of shadow, which helps to weight the image in space. Notice too how using only the smallest amount of bright white is necessary for all the accompanying areas to be read as white. If bright white had been used solidly throughout, this would have given a flattening effect, and you would have had less of an impression of the form of the shell. Use these ideas to give your mosaic a three-dimensional feel (see Three-dimensional Effects, page 126).

SETTING UP

Types of Tesserae

The various types of tesserae available for mosaic work have specific characteristics. This section is a guide to tesserae, looking into their suitability for different locations as well as the sizes, availability, and relative cost of the materials.

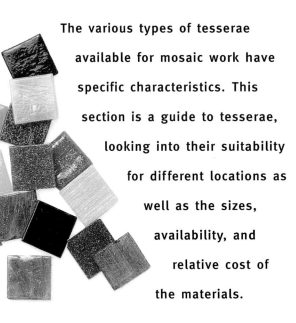

Vitreous glass is the most colorful mosaic medium in which to work but it is not generally suitable for use on floors. Unglazed ceramic is sufficiently hardwearing to use on floors but comes in a more limited range of muted colors. Glazed ceramic comes in brighter colors but, because it is colored only on one side, it is difficult to use with the indirect method (see pages 92–95). Marble has a natural color range and tends to be thicker than other materials, making it difficult to use in some locations. Gold and silver are dazzling and luxurious but also expensive.

Each material has different properties which will affect how you use it and what your design can look like. The important thing about mosaic-making is not to see these properties as limitations but to follow what the medium offers and to allow the materials to inspire you in ways which you may not otherwise have considered.

☞
Color in mosaics,
pages 18–25
Cutting techniques,
pages 66–69

◄ **UNGLAZED CERAMIC**
Unglazed ceramic tiles are hard-wearing and frost-proof. They are particularly suitable for use on floors. The color range is generally earthy and muted. They are probably the easiest of mosaic materials to cut. They come in single color sheets from the factory, 14 x 14in. The tiles are around 1in square and $1/_8$in thick. They can also be bought loose, or in random mixes of colors. Unglazed ceramic is probably the cheapest of the ready-made mosaic materials.

► **VITREOUS GLASS**
This material offers the widest range of colors. Vitreous glass is supplied from the factory in single color sheets 12 x 12in, and the tiles are $1/_8$in thick. If you immerse the sheet in warm water, the glue dissolves and the tiles float off the paper. They can then be dried and used for decorative work. It is also possible to buy mixed bags of tesserae, either in random mixes or tonal mixes. Vitreous glass is good for walls, ceilings, tables, and decorative objects. It is not ideal for floors, because it can break if subject to sharp and heavy forces. Cost depends somewhat on the degree of intensity of the color: bright colors, black, pink, and glass striated with metallic ores are the most expensive; whites and pale colors are the cheapest.

▶ GLAZED CERAMIC

The range of glazed ceramic mosaic tiles is limited—they are available mainly in blues, greens, and other colors that are considered suitable for swimming pools. They tend to be domed, which makes them difficult to use once they have been cut. The cost ranges from a price comparable to unglazed ceramic to a price comparable to that of glass.

▼ GLAZED CERAMIC TILES

Glazed ceramic wall and floor tiles can be cut and used for creative effect. High-fired floor tiles are more difficult to cut than crumbly, low-fired wall tiles. Keep in mind the fundamental strength of the tiles when you use them—do not assume that low-fired tiles will be suitable for use on floors if you cut them into smaller pieces. In fact, cutting any glazed tile is likely to reduce its strength, since you are interfering with the relationship between the glaze and the tile body. Soft wall tiles are often used externally, but you are taking a risk if you use them in works destined for installation outdoors because they are not designed to stand up to the elements. Glazed ceramic tiles are usually cheaper than unglazed mosaic.

▲ SMALTI

This is the material in which Byzantine mosaics were made. It is produced in cakes, often about 12in in diameter and is cut down from these into rectangular tesserae about $1/_3$in thick and about $2/_3$in long. Smalti is enameled glass and has enormous intensity of color. It is very expensive and not particularly easy to use. The glass is pitted with little holes and is traditionally left ungrouted because the holes fill up with grout, muting the vibrancy of color. Smalti is only used for walls and small decorative pieces, since its fractured face and pitted body make it unsuitable for floors.

▲ MARBLE

Many of the oldest mosaics were made from marble and other local stones. The natural variation within a single color gives marble its unique interest. Traditionally used for floors, it can also be used on walls. However because it is fairly thick, generally a minimum of $1/3$in, it is heavy, making it slightly tricky to fix in place. Unlike other mosaic materials, a single piece can be cut and finished in a variety of ways. Marble is expensive, but not as expensive as smalti. It is available in a variety of different finishes.

HONED MARBLE

Marble can be honed by grinding it to a fairly high polish, stopping short of producing a glassy finish. This brings out the color of the stone but produces a matte rather than a reflective surface, giving the marble a more natural appearance.

RIVEN MARBLE

Marble can also be riven. This is a term used to describe breaking open the cube to reveal its crystalline inner body. Riven marble has an interesting textured quality.

▶ POLISHED MARBLE

Marble can be polished, revealing its body color through a glassy finish. Polished marble is generally supplied in mosaic tiles known as cubes. These can be purchased loose or in sheet form. When it is in sheets, it is often stuck to the mesh with waterproof glue, so it is safer to buy a mix of marble cubes than to risk being unable to soak the marble off the mesh.

◄ MARBLE RODS

In order to create cubes, marble tiles are first cut into lengths known as rods. These can be cut down further with a marble saw (a large piece of equipment, not generally needed by the amateur mosaicist) or more usually with a pair of tile cutters or a hammer and hardy (see page 68). These lengths of marble can also be used as they are, offering a contrast of scale. They are a cheaper way of buying marble.

▼ MIRROR MOSAIC

Mirror mosaic can be purchased in two forms. Fabric-backed sheets are supplied with a special adhesive that does not interfere with the silvering on the back of the mirror glass. Bought like this, the tesserae are relatively inexpensive. It does have a disadvantage. In order to produce the material, a single sheet of glass is cut in two directions with a grinding wheel, which leaves behind a ground score mark. When you use mirror tiles in sheet form, the score lines give an impression of grout lines. However, if you try to use them individually, you will find that each tile is fouled at its edge by the score marks. For this kind of use, individually cut mirror tiles, comparable in size to vitreous glass tiles, are better. These are more expensive, but they have no score marks.

◄ STAINED GLASS

Stained glass can be used in mosaic. It is easier to find an application for opaque stained glass, but even transparent glass can be used in some projects. Cut the glass into strips with a glass cutter, and cut into mosaic pieces with tile cutters.

◀ GOLD AND SILVER
Tesserae in gold, silver, and a range of metallic colors are produced in Italy. They are generally available in $^3/_4$ in tile size. The tiles laid with gold or silver leaf coated with a thin skin of glass to protect the leaf. They are extremely expensive.

▼ PEBBLES
Marble pebbles are very soft and can be easily cut. Because they are so soft, they are best suited to interior use. Small stones and pebbles make wonderful mosaic materials and can be a souvenir of places you have visited. Do not remove stones from nature reserves or other protected environments without prior permission.

▼ FOUND OBJECTS
Many other materials can also be used in mosaic—you are only limited by your imagination. Consider using old jewelry, shells, sequins, or even guitar picks. The most unorthodox items can work if you find a creative way to incorporate them into a design.

► BROKEN CHINA

Every household has access to broken china at some point. However, it is important to be as selective about textures and colors as you would be if you had purchased the material.

Safety Equipment

Whenever you work with sharp tools, chemical preparations, or materials that can shatter, as you do in mosaic-making, it is essential to take safety precautions. This is especially important if you try to encourage friends or children to share your enthusiasm. It is easier to get others to take safety seriously if you do so yourself.

REMEMBER

Do
- always take safety precautions, even if you are only working for a short time.
- clear up between mosaic-making sessions, otherwise children or animals might hurt themselves on the debris.

Don't
- become complacent about safety as you get more experienced in mosaic-making. Even experienced mosaicists still suffer from splinters!
- pick up the debris left after cutting tiles with your bare hands. Use a dustpan and brush every time.
- let animals into a room where you are making a mosaic.

BUCKETS
Do not clean your tools or other equipment in a domestic sink or pour the remnants of your fixing materials, such as water containing grout and adhesive, down the drain. These materials contain cement, and they can set even under water, so you will be endangering your plumbing and drainage systems if you do so. Instead, keep a bucket or small garbage pail as a slops container. It only takes a day or so for the solids in the water to separate. You can then pour the clear water down the drain and decant the solids into a plastic bag, which you can put out with the garbage.

RUBBER GLOVES
Cement or any substance containing cement is very harsh and drying for the skin. It is also a potential allergen. Wear gloves whenever you use cement, cement-based adhesives, or grouts containing cement.

KNEEPADS

There is a construction site truism that goes, "You never see an old tiler." If you spend any time making a mosaic floor, you will soon recognize the truth in the saying. You can, however, take measures to protect your knees. Kneepads are the usual choice, although some people find them uncomfortable. A good alternative is a small rubber or polystyrene cushion, as used by gardeners. This will also protect your knees from the dampness of the floor.

MASK

Always wear a mask when cutting mosaic. If you sit in a sunny spot while cutting, you can see the amount of dust that is thrown up every time you fracture a tile. If you inhale this over long periods, it will affect your lungs. The dust from marble tiles is especially harmful. People who wear glasses find it difficult to wear masks, because they tend to steam up. Try a variety of masks until you find one that does not have this effect, rather than abandoning the idea. Also wear a mask for mixing grout, adhesive, or anything containing cement.

GOGGLES

It is advisable to protect your eyes from tiny splinters of material that may be thrown up when you are cutting. If you already wear glasses with reinforced plastic lenses, it is not generally necessary to take further protective measures.

Drawing Equipment

Not all of these tools are necessary for the beginner, but as you tackle larger and more ambitious projects you will find uses for many of them. For more information about design, turn to design sources (pages 14–17), design techniques (pages 70–73), and taking templates (pages 122–125).

REMEMBER

Do
- take into account the size and color of the tiles you are going to use when you are planning your design.
- be flexible when laying your design out in tiles. Good designs will evolve as you work.

Don't
- abandon a design idea if it doesn't work first time. Try redrawing it, simplifying it, or using different colors.

BROWN PAPER
This is the paper on which all indirect method papered-up mosaic is laid. Make sure you use a heavy grade of paper—42 lbs is ideal. Thinner papers do not take the weight of heavy mosaic materials as easily and are more likely to stretch. Thicker papers take a long time to absorb moisture when it is time to peel them off and also have a tendency to layer. Make sure your paper is not waxed, because waxed paper is resistant to absorbing moisture.

LAYOUT PAPER
This is drawing paper that is thin enough to allow you to see through it. It is useful for working out designs. If, for instance, you have a design that is largely successful, but with some problematic elements, you can copy the elements you find satisfactory by placing a sheet of layout paper on top of the original drawing, and rework the areas that require further attention. Although it is thin, layout paper is sturdy enough to be used for presentation drawings.

CRAYONS
Select a range of crayons or colored pencils that represent the colors you will be using in mosaic. The more accurate you can make your preliminary drawing, the more useful it will be to you in solving potential problems.

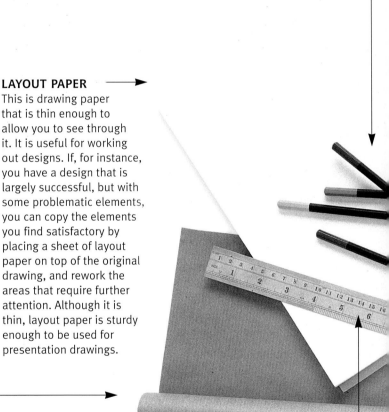

STRAIGHT EDGE
A long ruler or straight edge is another fundamental workshop item. It is necessary for creating large mosaic templates. A long, straight piece of wood is handy, but be aware that a length of timber that it can warp in time. A wobbly edge, particularly when you are planning to join your mosaic with sheeted-up material, will create problems.

CHARCOAL

Because you can easily rub charcoal out with the back of your hand, it is invaluable when you are creating designs —the knowledge that the marks you are making need only be temporary can encourage a freer and more confident approach.

Charcoal will be displaced by your brush as you apply glue onto the drawn surface, often turning the glue a dirty gray. However, this does not have a lasting effect on the mosaic.

COMPASSES

A beam compass is useful for drawing large circles for decorative circular panels. If it is beyond your budget, you can do a reasonable job with a long nail and some string to which you attach a pencil. Compasses are essential if you wish to draw fan designs (see page 120).

TRACING PAPER

It is easiest, although more expensive, to use it from a roll where you are not limited by the paper size, rather than in sheet form. The cheaper alternative is to stick sheets of tracing paper together using masking tape.

CRAFT KNIFE

This is an invaluable tool both in the workshop and when you are drawing designs. A sharp blade can cut through thick card without creating the slight wobbles along its edge that scissors inevitably produce.

PENCILS

It is useful to keep a variety of both hard and soft pencils. Soft pencils are easiest to use when developing a design, and hard ones are good when you need an accurate record of a design you have finished.

RIGHT ANGLE

If you are making a decorative feature in a field of sheeted-up mosaic, it is essential that the edges are straight and that the corners are at true 90 degree angles to one another. Any inaccuracies will create unsightly gaps. Getting an accurate right angle is almost impossible without a set square.

Surfaces

It is important to select the right surface for the right application, and this guide should help you to do so. The key issues are whether the surface will be exposed to water and how much weight can be supported.

REMEMBER

Do
- make sure your surface is clean and grease-free before you start.
- check if your surface needs to be sanded and primed, to allow adhesives to grip the surface properly.

GLASS AND MIRROR GLASS

It is possible to fix to glass if you use the correct adhesives. This can give new applications for mosaic, as window lights for example. Glass can also be useful when you require a surface that is thin but stable.

MASTERBOARD

A stable material in wet conditions, masterboard can even be immersed in water and remain sound. If you want to use it under water, you should fix it in position, or it will float to the top.

TILE BACKER BOARD

A fairly new product on the market, this is an ideal surface for mosaic. It is light, and can be used in wet areas, both internal and external. It is made for use with cement-based adhesives. It is not suitable for floors.

PARTICLE BOARD (Medium density fiberboard or MDF)

This is a very stable and inexpensive fixing surface. It is a good surface for small panels and interior tabletops. However, it is heavy and difficult to fit in screws and fixings. Do not use it outside or in wet areas, because if it comes into contact with water, it will swell up, throwing off the tiles. Always wear a mask when you cut it because the dust is said to be carcinogenic.

PLYWOOD

This is another good surface for interior mosaic. Marine ply can be used outside, but even this can layer if water penetrates if non-water-resistant fixings have been used.

SAND AND CEMENT

This is really the most adaptable surface there is, cheap, easy to make up, and flexible. You can make it fit the requirements of your site, feathering it (gradually laying it thinner) up to an edge, or making it really thick to cover all sorts of peculiarities beneath. A screed (a sand-and-cement bed laid on a floor) should not be less than about $^1/_2$in thick, and a rendered wall (a wall covered in sand and cement) should generally have an expanded metal lath (EML) fixed beneath it to protect the mosaic from any movement that may occur. Although it is very heavy, there is no sounder surface for exterior table tops. It is also ideal for cast slabs, for which you will need a casting frame, as shown here.

OTHER SURFACES

Using the right adhesives and primers, it is possible to fix mosaic to metal, terrazzo, fiberglass, and a whole variety of non-standard surfaces. Check the manufacturer's recommendations.

Adhesives

Selecting the right adhesive is the key to making a mosaic long-lasting. Check the manufacturer's recommendations to ensure that the one you wish to use is appropriate for the location in which you plan to use it.

CEMENT-BASED ADHESIVE

There are a wide variety of cement-based adhesives on the market. Think about the characteristics you need your adhesive to have and choose accordingly. There are quick-setting adhesives, which might be useful if you are fixing to plaster or another material that should not have prolonged exposure to moisture. Some adhesives are better at sticking to wood than others. Some adhesives also have different sensitivities to temperature.

REMEMBER

Do
- work in a well-ventilated space when using cement- or solvent-based adhesives.
- check the manufacturer's instructions on all adhesives. You must use an adhesive that is suited to the chosen surface.

- ask your local hardware store for advice on adhesives, particularly if you are unsure about certain properties.

Don't
- apply too much adhesive when you are laying mosaic tiles. If you apply too much adhesive it will squeeze up around the sides of the tile.

SAND AND CEMENT

Sand and cement is a highly adaptable adhesive. This is also probably the least expensive of all adhesives.

Lime is sometimes added to slow down the curing time, but this can be dangerous for the amateur to use.

BUILDING SILICONE
This is an excellent adhesive, although it has an unpleasant odor. Building silicone is useful for fixing mirror glass, because it does not interfere with the silvering.

WHITE CRAFT GLUE
There are two kinds of white craft glue, both invaluable for mosaic-making. Water-soluble white craft glue is used as a holding medium when you are working in reverse. You should mix it half and half with water. If you use it unmixed, the work will still come off the paper, but it leaves plastic-type deposits on the face of the mosaic, which are time-consuming to remove. It is also sometimes known as washable white craft glue.

Non-water-soluble white craft glue is used for panels and decorative pieces indoors. Do not apply it so thickly that it squeezes up between the joints in the mosaic, because it can yellow as it dries. Wipe away any that you accidentally smear on the face of the tiles.

There is also a permanent white craft glue suitable for exterior use. Do not use it as a fixing medium when you are using the indirect method, because it sets so fast that you cannot subsequently remove the backing paper.

Fixing Equipment

A variety of tools are required for fixing mosaics. Each different type of job requires its own special tools. Here is a brief description of each tool, and you will find more detailed explanations in the descriptions of mosaic techniques.

REMEMBER

Do
- use the right tool for the job. You may have to invest some money when you start but having the right tools will save you time in the long run.

Don't
- cut your tiles or tesserae over the prepared surface because any dust or dirt on the surface will make adhesive and grout fix less securely.

GLASS CUTTERS
These are useful for scoring straight lines, particularly on gold or silver tiles where mistakes can be expensive. They are also useful for cutting stained glass.

PAINTBRUSHES
For gluing, sealing, and painting, it is helpful to have a range of sizes. Stiffer, rather than softer, bristles are better for gluing.

TROWEL
For mixing adhesive, a flat-ended trowel gives you easy access to the edge of the bucket, which would be more difficult with a curved trowel.

STRAIGHT EDGE
Use a length of timber that is truly straight, in combination with a level, to check the condition of large surfaces.

TAPE MEASURE
It is worth investing in a large, sturdy tape measure, because you will use it constantly.

CARBORUNDUM
Use this to abrade uneven areas in a screed or render. This tool helps to create a flatter surface. For finer surfaces use a finer grade of Carborundum.

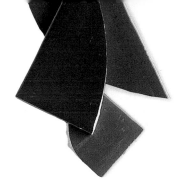

CARPENTER'S LEVEL

Few walls or floors are truly flat. If you are making a mosaic based on straight-laid tiles in which the grout lines run through in both directions, every inconsistency in the surface beneath will be reflected. You can at least ensure your mosaic is straight by using a level.

DUSTPAN AND BRUSH

This has obvious uses in a workshop, but it is also an essential piece of equipment when you are fixing mosaic. Every surface you fix to needs to be as clean and dust-free as possible—even the smallest amount of unwanted material can keep the tiles from bonding properly.

CRAFT KNIFE AND SCISSORS

These are essential equipment in the workshop. Keep the blades sharp.

SCREWDRIVERS

For everything from changing a craft knife blade to removing a door, screwdrivers in a range of sizes and types always come in handy.

HAMMER AND CHISEL

These are used to remove tiles that have adhered to a substrate. Use one that has a cutting blade appropriate for the size of tile you are removing.

TILE CUTTERS

These are essential for the mosaicist. See cutting techniques (pages 66–69) for more detail.

BUCKETS

Whenever you fix mosaic, you will need at least one bucket to hold the water for cleaning your tools and rinsing out your sponge. For larger projects, they are also essential for mixing grout and adhesive.

Grouting Equipment

Fixing and grouting are part of the same process, but grouting requires a range of specialist equipment. The larger the mosaic panel that you are making, the more you will appreciate how these tools will speed up your work.

REMEMBER

Do
- mix a large enough quantity of grout for your whole project.
- make notes on the quantity of any color added. The grout color will look different when dry, making it impossible to match the color unless you have taken accurate notes.

Don't
- pour unused grout down your sink or household drains.
- forget to wear rubber gloves to protect your skin from the harsh chemicals contained in grout. If you don't wear gloves you risk suffering from an allergic reaction or dry skin problems.

RAGS
Keep a collection of lint-free cloths, which are always useful in cleaning up mosaic after grouting.

SPONGE
A large but fine grained sponge is an essential mosaic tool. Adhesive manufacturers often produce very good ones. Do not leave them in water in which cement has dissolved, because cement ruins good sponges remarkably quickly.

SPATULA
Useful for any work on a very small scale, or when working on a curved surface.

WALLPAPER SCRAPER
This is an ideal tool for mixing grout. The flat-ended blade allows you to get right to the bottom of any bucket. They are inexpensive and easily available.

GROUTING SQUEEGEES
These come in a variety of sizes and weights. For small projects, a cheap squeegee from a hardware store is adequate. For small panels and uneven surfaces, it is often just as easy to push the grout into place with your hand as it is to grout with a squeegee (you should wear rubber gloves to do this). A good basic squeegee is strong, fairly cheap, and long-lasting. Its flexible rubber blade makes it slightly easier to use than the cheaper, more rigid ones. Although they are expensive, it is worth spending the money. Using one of these, you can grout a wall in about a quarter of the time it takes with a rubber-bladed squeegee.

GROUT
Grout is a mixture of cement and fine sand. Manufacturers produce grout for both wide and narrow joints. Wide-joint grout uses a coarser grade of sand and is easier to use and less slimy than that used for narrow joints. Grout is widely available in a variety of colors, and admixes can be added to white grout to produce less traditional colors. Epoxy grout is more water-resistant than normal grout and is often recommended for outdoor use. It is more difficult to use than cement-based grout, and considerably more expensive.

Workshop Set-up

As with any craft, it is important to work in the correct environment. It is ideal to have a workshop in your home dedicated to mosaic-making. If this is not possible, you can set up a temporary workspace, clearing up at the end of each day or once you have completed a project. Whether your work area is permanent or not, there are certain basic requirements.

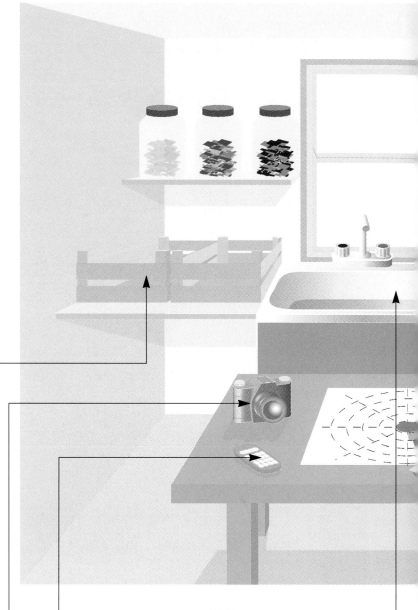

REMEMBER

Do
- make sure that you are comfortable with the workspace that you have for both work and storage.
- Keep all chemicals and additives used securely out of reach of children.

Don't
- work in a closed-up room. Ventilation is essential because cutting tesserae produces dust and the chemicals in grout can often be very strong.

STORAGE UNITS FOR MOSAIC
Once you have built up a reasonable quantity of stock, you may need to think of creative ways to store your supplies. A cheap and effective way is to store material in fruit boxes. These can be stacked on one another, so they are economical with space. Remember to attach samples of the tiles to the outside, so you can see at a glance which box you need.

CAMERA
This is obviously required to keep a portfolio of finished pieces. It is also useful to keep a record of color experiments and works in progress.

CALCULATOR
This is essential for working out areas and for pricing work.

SINK
It is not essential to have a water supply in the room, but it certainly is useful to have one close at hand, because many mosaic-making processes require water.

SHELVING

Shelving is an accessible way of storing mosaic materials, because you can see your supplies easily. The colors of the materials themselves can often be inspiring.

SOAKING TRAYS

You do not necessarily need special trays for soaking tiles off the paper sheets of factory-produced mosaic, but it is easier if the individual sheets are laid flat. It you put too many sheets into a tray together, the water cannot penetrate the paper and the glue does not release, so only soak a few sheets at a time. It is more time-consuming to put sheets of different colors in a tray together, because you will need to separate the colors afterwards. Do not stack wet tiles on top of one another, as they often have residual amounts of glue left on their face from the paper and will stick together again as they dry.

TOOLBOX

Always put your tools in the toolbox and then you will know where they are when you next need them. Keep them out of the reach of children. Remember that some tools are expensive and therefore valuable, so they should be kept in a secure place.

PORTFOLIO

Keeping a portfolio of photographs of your work is a useful discipline. Try to keep a record right from the start. Even if you feel embarrassed about your early pieces, it is encouraging to keep a record of your progress. A portfolio is also useful if you want to show people the kinds of work you can do for commissions.

A LARGE TABLE IN WELL-LIT POSITION

Mosaic-making must take place somewhere really well-lit, ideally with natural light. You need to be sure your work can stand up to close scrutiny, and that any color decisions you make are based on an accurate impression.

A TO Z OF
MOSAIC
TECHNIQUES

Adhesive Techniques

Adhesive is the medium with which you fix the tiles. The ones most frequently used by interested amateurs are those based on plastic (such as white craft glue), which are easy to use direct and tend to be less messy than those derived from sand and cement (see Direct Method).

It is worth familiarizing yourself with sand-and-cement based adhesives, however, since they are much more adaptable than plastic-based ones. They are simple to use on vertical surfaces, or even on a ceiling, because they have a great deal of grip. For this reason, they are commonly used for architectural mosaics. They also have body, which allows you to even out the differences between thicker and thinner tiles. Remember, it is essential to wear rubber gloves when working with cement-based adhesives.

YOU WILL NEED

Tools
Grouting squeegee
⅛in notched trowel
Flat-ended mixing trowel
   for mixing adhesive
Wallpaper scraper for
   mixing grout
Bucket
Sponge
Rubber gloves
Small tool

Materials
Grout
Adhesive
Board onto which mosaic
   will be fixed
Tiles

1 Mix the powdered grout with water to a fairly stiff mix, and put to one side. Choose a cement-based adhesive suitable to the job— check the manufacturer's recommendations. For example, not all cement-based adhesives work well on wood; some require special admixes or that you prime the board first. Mix the cement-based adhesive with water, carefully following the instructions. Once both grout and adhesive are ready, pre-grout the mosaic from the back.

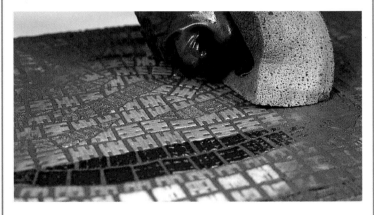

2 Sponge any excess grout from the back of your piece with a damp, but thoroughly squeezed-out sponge. Clean off with the sponge flat on the mosaic, wiping in a series of broad sweeps. Dabbing at the mosaic will not clean it properly.

☞
**Direct method, pages 74–77
Tesserae, pages 28–33**

6 Wet the back thoroughly with a sponge, and leave to absorb the moisture for a good five minutes. If the paper has not turned dark brown or there are paler patches evident on the paper, continue wetting.

3 This technique is not necessary in all cases, but it is a useful one to know. Tiles produced by different manufacturers are sometimes of different thicknesses, leaving you with an uneven surface. However, by "buttering" the back of the tiles, you can compensate for any unevenness and thus produce a flat surface. Simply apply extra adhesive to the areas where the tiles are thinner, taking the surface up to the level of the thickest tile.

7 Once the paper has changed color to a really dark brown, peel it off. Remember to pull the paper back on itself, not upward, or you may displace tiles. If any tiles should accidentally come away, simply replace them in their original position. If it looks as if there is no adhesive in the gap, put a small quantity on the back of the tile before placing it in the hole.

4 Once the levels have been evened out, apply adhesive to the board with a notched trowel. Flatten the trowel slightly to apply adhesive, but use it at a 90-degree angle to remove any excess. Try to make sure there is an even quantity across the whole surface. If some areas don't have enough adhesive, the tiles will not stick.

5 Carefully, without folding or flapping it, turn over the mosaic panel. Aligning the corners with the corners of the board, place it in position. Give the back of the mosaic a gentle tap to ensure it is all in contact with the adhesive.

8 Once the paper has been removed, sponge the mosaic from the front. It need not be perfectly clean, but make sure there are no lumps in the grout before it dries. Once the mosaic has had time to dry and is thoroughly set, regrout from the front.

For the finished item, see Design Techniques, page 71.

Andamenti

Andamenti is a term used in mosaic-making which refers to the coursing of the grout lines—the way in which the flow of the lines helps to give form to the work. There are many different andamenti techniques, and many are named (see Opus for more information on the frequently used ones).

Andamenti is about introducing a system to your work. Once you have decided how the andamenti will flow in your piece, it is important to be consistent. Like all systems of rules, it may provide restrictions, but it also allows a kind of freedom within its boundaries. This panel of pigeons in a pear tree demonstrates the ways in which andamenti can be used to enhance your work.

The panel is laid by running lines of tiles across the design. These tiles stay in line even when the design elements change, giving a feeling of harmony. Some systems of laying tiles are lively and add a feeling of movement to a piece. The purpose of this system is to give an impression of calm.

> ☞
> **Laying techniques,
> pages 98–101
> Opus, pages 104–111**

▲ Occasionally you can emphasize a particular design feature by breaking your own rule. This leaf is a case in point. The upper part of the leaf runs into the main grout lines. You can see the way the tiles are broken so that the upper side of the leaf and the background express the same line. However the left side of the leaf breaks this rule and has a more expressive, leaf-like quality by doing so. The way the tiles suddenly run at a different angle makes the leaf look genuinely veined.

▲ Here the neck of the pigeon runs into the grout lines of the background at an angle, helping to express the plump form of the bird. Just to the right of the pigeon is another leaf, which makes an interesting comparison with the top picture. Here the lines run straight through and the leaf is less animated.

◄ These bright patches of color work because the eye makes sense of areas of intense brightness around the bird's neck. Once again, note how the changing direction of the andamenti help to describe the form of the bird.

► This picture gives an impression of the way in which most of the background is laid. However the structure, the bare bones of the design against which the rest is defined, is the heavier, darker tones of the branches. To give these further emphasis, they are laid in a way that breaks the overall andamenti pattern.

► The feathers on the pigeons' wings employ the same system of lining through the grout lines. This helps to create an authentic impression of the way feathers fold up against one another. Note the way in which a feeling of form is given by minor variations in tone.

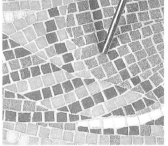

▼ This bird's head is the most impressionistic element in the piece. The grout lines run through so the form is created by variations in color. The bird's beak breaks the andamenti system, giving emphasis to this key feature.

► The main field of this design is laid in lines that run all the way through the objects, from side to side. This is not a typical mosaic way of working, and there is no special name for it. It gives a flat, harmonious quality to a finished surface. If you are going to work like this, you have to be very disciplined about making your cuts run along the lines, and it can take a lot of experimentation to find the most elegant way to do it.

Backgrounds

Mosaic backgrounds can be laid in an infinite variety of ways. How the tiles flow around an image alters the way in which you read it. If the background tiles follow the direction in which the central design is laid, it can give quite a lively sense of movement.

If, on the other hand, the background tiles are laid as regular straight lines, the main image can be made to look rather static. With a very graphic or stylized piece the background treatment can be an intrinsic part of the mosaic, and there may be no clear point of division between background and foreground.

The background should be thought of as an intrinsic part of the whole mosaic piece, rather than simply an empty area that needs to be filled in order to complete the mosaic. By thinking of the background in this way you are likely to come across much more imaginative solutions and discoveries. Think of the variety of background texture you can create with a pencil—when you cross hatch, or sketch in different directions, building up a description of form through thicker and thinner, darker and lighter lines—and translate this to your mosaic design.

The following panels are practice pieces made to illustrate some interesting approaches to the background. When you are producing mosaics where there are large areas of background, it is worth carrying out experiments like these. Some designs can bear quite a strong tonal and color field. For others a strong background would be far too dominating. Suit your approach to the requirements of the design. One of the most enjoyable aspects of inventing new background treatments is that you can give a free rein to your instinct to be playful.

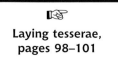

☞
**Laying tesserae,
pages 98–101**

▲ This is probably the simplest way of dealing with a background, and it means you can use factory-prepared, sheeted-up mosaic. In this instance, the stark, straight-laid, simple background actually emphasizes the naturalistic feel of the treatment, and the grout lines help to accentuate the veining of the moths' wings.

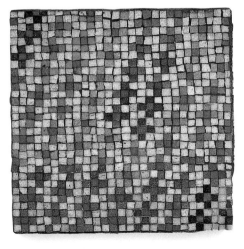

◄ This design builds an interesting background from a simple repeat. The tiles have been quarter-cut and are arranged in vertical and horizontal lines, but tiny elements of distortion have been introduced to enliven the effect. The design has been given complexity and interest by the variety of slight color changes within the repeat, and by the use of roughly cut tiles, which means that the eye does not immediately grasp the pattern. A pattern without much variation will not hold our attention for long.

▲ This panel continues to experiment with the pattern repeat, but introduces a new idea of subdividing areas through more strongly differing colors. The effect gives the mosaic a layered look.

▲ Here, the panel illustrates how you can give interest to a repeating pattern through minute distortions. The curved lines that the color changes follow, and the wavy distortion created by using tiles of slightly differing shapes and sizes, make the basic geometric pattern appear to flow like fabric.

▲ The simple theme can be infinitely varied. Once you have come up with an idea, be prepared to pursue it; often it does require a bit of work to discover what can really be done with it. Here, the basic theme has been worked to make the color contrasts bolder but the distortion of shape more subtle.

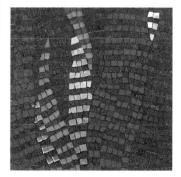

◄ This mosaic is laid along one, essentially horizontal, undulating line. The tonal closeness makes the background quite subtle, but the distortions and variations of vertical shapes give it interest. Some silver mosaic has been used to introduce a reflective element to the design.

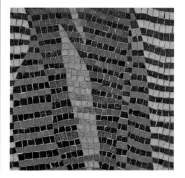

◄ In this instance, more sharply contrasting tones have been used. Once again there is a sense of layering, which can help to give an impression of depth, an element far too often ignored in mosaic. People are often tempted to use single flat color as background, but this approach really wastes the potential of mosaic.

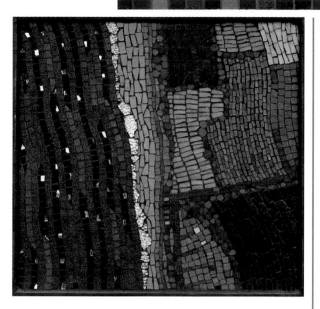

▲ In this panel the whole design, which is an aerial view of a coastline, is treated with equal interest and the result is a very rich feel to the mosaic.

▲ This whole piece was made with a view to pattern, line, and tone. A variety of laying techniques and changing angles have been used, making this mosaic playful and experimental, and therefore enjoyable to look at.

Borders

Some borders are geometric, others take a freer approach like the one shown here (left). The process of creating a traditional, repeating rope border illustrates many of the fundamental rules involved in making borders. The design is up to you. This border is designed to fit in with sheeted-up tiles.

It is perfectly possible to make a border which has no repeats. You can cut out a long strip of paper, draw your design onto it, and stick it directly to the paper. The border can be subdivided for fixing once it is completely laid in place. It is necessary to number the sections and make a key drawing, otherwise it may not be obvious how to put the border back together again. There are no such problems with a repeating border though. This section shows how to make one.

1 Whether or not you are designing your own border, one decision is critical, and that is the size of the tile you are using. This is known as the tile module. In order to make a design flow elegantly, and to minimize cutting, it is a good idea to base the width of the border on the module. In addition, if your border is designed to fit in with sheeted-up material, you need to make it the exact width of a series of tiles—in other words, the top and bottom of the border must be located at the exact spot where joints run in the sheeted-up material. Otherwise, you will have to cut tiles on the sheet, either on the inside or the outside.

2 Once you have selected the tiles you wish to use and have decided on the tile module, measure out an area that matches sheet joints both horizontally and vertically. Divide the area into lines that represent the coursing of the mosaic tiles. Divide this into four sections representing the places where the high and low points of your design will fall.

3 Draw the design freehand onto the paper: use layout paper, so you can redraw the design if necessary without having to take measurements all over again. Sketch on the paper with charcoal initially, as this is easily erased if you make a mistake.

YOU WILL NEED
Tools
Ruler
Pencil
Charcoal
Crayons

Materials
Layout paper
Brown paper
Water-soluble white craft glue
A selection of mosaic tiles

☞
Indirect method, pages 92–95
Taking templates, pages 122–125

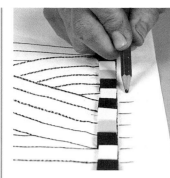

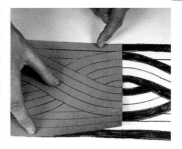

4 Once you have established the basic shape of the border, redraw it showing the way in which you plan to course the tiles. Remember, the tiles must meet each end at exactly the same spot, or the border will not align correctly.

6 Color in your drawing. It is useful to file this away once the mosaic is completed, keeping it as a template in case you want to use the same border again in the future.

7 Draw the design onto brown paper. Because the design is geometrically constructed, it offers a further potential repeat break in the center. If you have not made the length of the border match an even number of tiles on a sheet, using this repeat will mean having to cut tiles on the sheeted-up material.

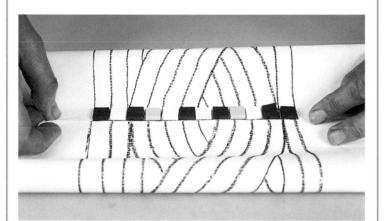

5 Once you have drawn the coursing, check that both ends meet precisely. You can do so by folding the paper over and onto itself.

8 Following your colored drawing, stick the tiles to the brown paper. This is your border section. You can proceed with grouting and fixing it in place by the indirect method (see pages 92–95).

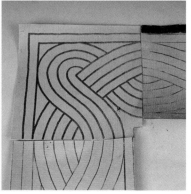

9 Corners obey the same rules as borders and can be made following the same principles.

Casting

It can be hazardous to place an uneven piece on a floor. This technique is ideal when you need to produce something flat for practical reasons but want to use materials of different depths. By sticking the mosaic to paper, you automatically create one reasonably flat plane.

This is the finished face. You then cast sand and cement on top of it, disguising the differences in height. Large pieces need a thick fixing bed, so you can end up with something weighty and substantial. Such mosaics are not suitable everywhere but can be very effective used in the garden. The slab here is made in a square frame, but the same principles apply for all shapes.

YOU WILL NEED

Tools
Screwdriver
Scissors
Sponge
Paintbrush
Rubber gloves
Grouting squeegee
Wallpaper scraper
Flat bed squeegee
2 large boards

Materials
Casting frame (4 pieces of batten, 8 screws, backing board)
Water-soluble white craft glue
Petroleum jelly
Brown paper
Charcoal
Expanded metal lath (EML) or chicken wire
Tiles, terra-cotta tiles, marble cubes, or any selection of materials you wish to use
Plastic sheeting
Cement
Sand

1 Make or buy a casting frame. To make one, screw four pieces of batten to a backing board. Do not use glue because it is essential to be able to dismantle it later. Ensure a tight fit between the battens so there will be no leakage from the joints.

2 Cut a piece of paper slightly smaller than the internal dimension of your frame. The gap you leave will be at the edge of the tiles, and you will fill this with cement.

☞
Indirect method on paper, pages 92–95
Cutting techniques, pages 66–69

3 Draw your design onto the paper with charcoal. The charcoal can be rubbed off easily if you need to amend the design slightly.

4 | Stick the mosaic to the paper using a water-soluble white craft glue, diluted 50:50 with water (see Indirect Method). Ensure that the gap you leave between the tiles is similar throughout. You may need to cut tiles to accomplish this (see Cutting Techniques). When it is complete, let it dry thoroughly.

5 | Use a sponge to spread petroleum jelly evenly and thoroughly over the inside of the frame. This acts as a release agent, ensuring the finished work will not stick to the surface of the wood.

6 | Place your mosaic into the base of the frame, paper side down. Do not bend or fold the paper as you transfer it, because this may cause tiles to peel away. If this occurs, reglue and leave to dry before pregrouting. This is your last chance to check the spacing between the tiles. Once the grout is applied, it will not be possible to make any changes.

7 | Terra-cotta absorbs water from cement, causing it to crumble and not set properly. To prevent this, wet any terracotta tiles by brushing water over them.

8 | Pregrout. Mix a cement slurry (a creamy mixture of cement and water) and apply it with a squeegee to the back of the mosaic. Push it into all the joints, and scrape off any excess. Always wear gloves when working with cement.

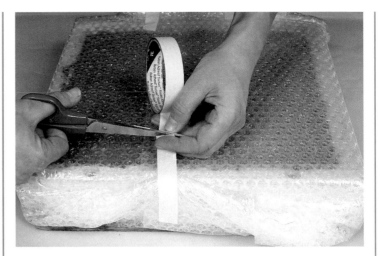

9 | Mix together one part cement to three parts sand. Add water until the mixture is firm but workable, with no water running out of it. Apply a layer of this to the back of the tiles using a wallpaper scraper. About halfway up the frame, smooth the mixture.

11 | Smooth down the surface with a flat bed squeegee. It can sometimes be useful to inscribe information into this wet mix, such as the ambient temperature of the workroom or details of how you made the piece. This is especially helpful if you are doing something unusual, using a different kind of sand for example, and want to replicate it later.

12 | Wrap the slab in plastic sheeting. Leave it to set for at least a week.

10 | Place a piece of expanded metal lath (EML) or chicken wire on top of the sand and cement mix. This will give your slab strength. Apply a second layer of sand and cement until it reaches the top of the frame. You should not be able to see any EML. If you can see any, remove the sand and cement, relay the EML, and cover once again.

13 | Unwrap the slab carefully. Unscrew each batten and remove it. When they are all off, place a board underneath and a board on top of the mosaic, sandwich them tightly together, and turn over. Be careful to maintain a tight grip while you do this. Remove the board. You should now be able to see the paper.

14 Use a sponge to wet the paper thoroughly. Leave it for ten minutes to absorb the moisture, checking periodically that it is not drying out.

15 Peel the paper carefully away from the face of the mosaic. Try to keep it in a single piece, peeling from one corner to the center, then turning the slab around and working in from the other corner.

16 Regrout the front of the mosaic with a cement slurry made up as before. Make sure all the tiny holes are filled.

◄ The finished panel has a completely flat surface, making it safe to use on floors or in the garden.

17 Wet a clean sponge and squeeze out as much water as possible. Use this to clean your slab. Rewrap the slab in plastic and leave for two weeks to dry. The slab can then be laid in the garden.

Central Motifs

A central mosaic motif can be used to make a plain floor more lively. The key issues in making a central motif work in a mosaic floor are ones of color, scale, and practicality. It is essential to get the proportion and emphasis right.

This motif is made in vitreous glass, which is only suitable for use on bathroom floors or areas of light foot traffic. However, the principles apply to all work where you are fixing into ready-made sheeted-up mosaic. It is not always necessary, nor even desirable, to cover an entire floor with cut-piece mosaic. It is possible to overdo it. Making cut piece designs can take a long time too. Often it is just as effective to make a decorative panel for a floor and lay plain material around it. The sheeted-up mosaic tiles can simply be fixed in place according to the indirect method, and your central motif fixed in the same way. Some of the issues involved are explained here.

YOU WILL NEED
Tools
Ruler
Pencil
Crayons

Materials
Layout paper
Brown paper
Water-soluble white craft
    glue
A selection of mosaic tiles,
    sheeted-up for the floor
    and loose for the motif

☞
**Indirect method,
pages 92–95
Taking templates,
pages 122–125**

1 It is helpful to take the measurements of the area for which you are planning a mosaic. Using this information, produce a scale drawing of the room, and sketch your design onto the drawing. A design that works well on a piece of paper may seem small in the context of a room. The fish design shown at this scale is obviously not large enough to make much of an impact.

2 If your feature seems too small, redraw it to a larger scale. It might seem time-consuming to draw and redraw the design, but time spent at the planning stage speeds up production time and ensures pleasing results.

3 Most central motifs benefit from the addition of a border or decorative surround. A simple linear border like this one increases the visual impact without significantly increasing labor. A circular border, although very effective, would be much more labor-intensive to produce, because it would require a lot of cutting.

4 Select the palette of tiles you wish to use, keeping in mind your choice of background colors and the color of the grout.

5 Measure a piece of brown paper so that it fits precisely with the sheeted-up tiles. Draw the central motif onto brown paper, enlarging it if necessary (see Taking Templates). Where straight lines of tiles run through the whole design, it is helpful to use a straight edge or long ruler to draw guidelines, to prevent uneven gaps or crooked sections.

6 Lay the decorative element of the design first. When so much of the design is made from sheeted-up material, accuracy in cutting around the cut-piece motif is even more important.

7 Once the design is complete, recheck the accuracy of your straight lines before fixing the mosaic in position. It is essential that any inaccuracies are sorted out on paper before you fix, because troubleshooting at a later stage is much more difficult.

Common Mistakes

Many mosaicists fall prey to the same basic mistakes when they begin. This section is a guide to some of the most common pitfalls. By studying the ways in which other people have gone wrong, you will be able to avoid such mistakes yourself.

As you become more experienced as a mosaicist, you will develop your critical faculties. Things which previously pleased you may seem flawed with the benefit of hindsight. This can be true in both technical terms and also for aesthetic judgments.

The problems which are discussed here are not the finer points of design and cutting, which are skills that you will naturally develop over a period of time. Instead these tips concern some basic points of technical practice which it is possible to watch out for right from your first mosaic. Taking care in planning and paying attention to the details in all aspects of mosaic making will enable you to produce good quality mosaics.

▲ This is a mosaic of a cabbage, but the image is not clear because of two factors: the tiles are too similar in tone, and the grout is also a similar tone. It is generally effective to choose a grout that matches the predominant tone of your piece, but it can sometimes unite the piece excessively. An alternative would be to use a contrasting color, but that has a fracturing effect. The only other solution is more labor-intensive. If, during the laying process, your tones seem to be too close together, then change your tile colors. You probably only need to change one color to bring the piece to life.

☞

**Color in mosaics, pages 18–25
Indirect method, pages 92–95
Laying, pages 98–101
Three-dimensional surfaces, pages 128–129**

▶ The intricate cutting and sophisticated floral design of the border completely vanishes as the dark grout further unites its close tones. In addition, the dark grout is unattractive against the white tiles. If the mosaic had been grouted white, there would have been two consequences: the grout would have complemented and united the field color, because it would not have fractured the joints between the tiles; and the intricate border would have been more readable, with the colors heightened.

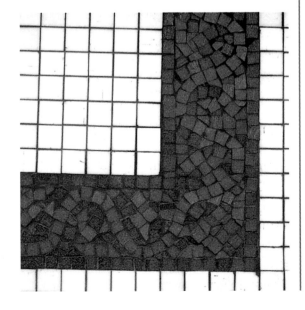

▲ This piece demonstrates another common grout error. In this mosaic, there is a high contrast between the white tiles and the dark ones making up the design and the background. A gray grout, rather than white, would have been more effective because it would have fractured both light and dark tones equally. Instead, the white tiles are united, making the dark ones look scrappy and chaotic. When you have high contrast in terms of tone, choose a grout in an intermediate tone that fractures both light and dark areas evenly.

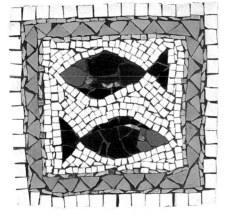

▲ This mosaic is an example of sloppy basic work. The board was not cut carefully, and the paper size was not checked. But it also demonstrates a less obvious problem. When sticking tiles to paper (see Indirect Method), it absorbs moisture from the glue and expands slightly; as it dries, it contracts again and the mosaic tiles are pulled together. If they are laid very closely they will not lie flat once the paper has contracted. They are likely to come unstuck. Even if they do stick to the paper, you may not be able to flatten them out later. Make sure you always leave an even gap of at least $1/_{32}$ inch between the tiles when sticking them to paper.

▲ If there was only one golden rule of mosaic making, it would be, "Don't Mosaic the Edge." Edges are intrinsically vulnerable, and mosaic applied to them almost invariably falls off. Do not put mosaic around the edge of a table, because it will fall off. Do not put mosaic around the edge of a panel, unless you never plan to move it again once it is on the wall. Do not apply mosaic to objects that you will move around and use on a regular basis. (See Finishing and Fixing for more information.)

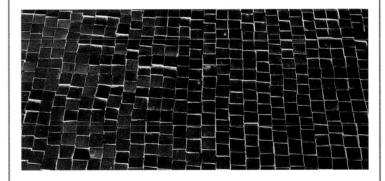

▲ This panel has two related problems, which both have to do with working on paper. First, the mosaic was obviously laid too tightly on the paper, which has prevented it from lying flat. Second, if you look in the center of the picture, you can see a sheet joint. Where the gaps are even, it is easy to disguise sheet joints, but where the mosaic is butted up very tight, such joints are difficult to hide. There is one other subtle fault with this mosaic. Although some effort has been put into off-setting most of the tiles, there are areas where some of the tiles suddenly run through geometrically, breaking the rhythm. It is important to be consistent in laying the tiles to achieve a harmonious effect.

Cutting Techniques

Not all materials cut in the same way. This section explains how and why they fracture in the way they do, and shows how best to make them do what you want. You will know you have mastered cutting when your piece looks as if it was easy to make. See the Gallery for examples of work that demonstrate all these cutting techniques.

You do not need to worry about absolute precision when cutting. When you look at an image made in mosaic, particularly one that depends on color, you tend to focus on the entire image, rather than the cutting. In many cases how you lay the tiles is more visually significant than the cutting technique. However, good cutting technique will allow you to create tesserae to fit your design and to make the most of different materials.

When buying a pair of tile cutters, make sure you ask for "side" tile or mosaic cutters. Other tools for cutting tiles do not work as effectively on mosaic materials. For safety, always wear a mask when cutting any material.

☞
**Types of tesserae,
pages 28–33**

CERAMIC AND GLASS MOSAIC TILES

Ceramic is probably the easiest materials to fracture, and you can buy special small square tiles for mosaic-making. Because they have a very flat face and an unreflective surface, you notice the effect of the cuts more than with any other material. You can use this to your advantage in designs that depend on cut effects.

1 A simple and effective way to use ceramic mosaic tiles is to quarter-cut them. Place the cutters on the edge of the tile, at 90 degrees to it, and press, holding the tile in your hand as you do so. Do not cut tiles over your mosaic, because fragments may stick to the board or paper and prevent proper bonding.

2 You can also experiment with more ambitious shapes. If you need a precise shape, it helps to sketch it onto the tile with a pencil. Place the cutters on the edge of the tile at the angle you need. If you want a curve, you may have to make a series of cuts, "nibbling" the tile. Remember to cut away from your curve, rather than into it.

3 | Glass can be quartered in the same way as ceramic. Place the tile cutters on the edge of the tile, at 90 degrees to it, and squeeze gently. After cutting glass, do not sweep up fragments with your fingers; the shards are sharp and dangerous so use a brush.

CIRCLES

Circles are very useful for key details in mosaics, such as eyes, and are not difficult to cut for yourself.

Everything you cut is produced from a series of small straight lines, even circles, as shown here. "Nibble" the edge of the tile away to create the circle.

TRIANGLES

Triangles are always difficult to produce accurately. There are two principal ways of making them, when working with glass, ceramic, gold, silver, and mirror (marble is an exception).

1 | When you cut from the corner across a tile using cutters, you are only likely to produce one workable triangle, rather than two, and this one is likely to require further "nibbling" into shape.

2 | Although your initial cut is made from the edge, for further trimming you can place the cutters right over the area you wish to cut. If you begin by putting the cutters too far over the tile, you are likely to shatter it entirely.

3 | More accurate triangles can be made using a glass cutter. This one has a scoring wheel and a snapping mechanism. Score the tile from corner to corner, pressing hard. If you do not press hard enough, you will have to repeat the scoring process. Multiple score lines are likely to make the cuts less accurate.

4 | Place the mosaic tile so the score line runs along the shaft of the glass cutter. Press gently but firmly. If you are too timid, you may crumble the corners off the tile. Once you have mastered this technique, you will produce very accurate triangles and can get two usable ones from a single tile.

MARBLE

Because it is the thickest of the mosaic materials, marble can be unpredictable and difficult to cut. The natural veining in the marble presents additional difficulties. Marble is sometimes smashed up from tiles with a conventional hammer, but this is a crude, wasteful method, which creates unattractive bruises in the material. It is more skilful to cut it with a sharp mosaic hammer. However, if you are working with ready-formed cubes, cutters may be the most practical option.

1 The veining and stresses that occur naturally within marble mean that it may crumble or fracture if you try to cut from the edge. Instead, place your tile cutters centrally along the line you wish to break and exert sharp pressure. If you try to cut too slowly, this can make the material crumble, and sorting out badly formed cuts is trickier with this material than with any other, not least because of its thickness.

2 Marble can have three main finishes: polished, honed, or riven (see Tesserae). Riven marble is created by a cutting process. Place a marble cube within the jaws of the cutters and exert sharp pressure. By cutting it in half, you create a rectangular rather than a square piece. Continue nipping down until you reach the desired shape.

3 Marble is available either in cubes or in rods. Rods are saw-cut from tiles and less expensive than cubes. They can be cut either with tile cutters or with a mosaic hammer. The effect of having two slightly irregular edges softens the machine-made finish. If the cutters will not open wide enough to take the depth of the marble, remove the spring, which is not essential for the cutters to function. This also helps if your hands are becoming blistered, often a hazard of working with marble.

4 The quickest way to make a simple, straightforward cut is with a hammer and hardy. The hammer ends with a pointed blade and is used in conjunction with a chisel-type blade, stuck in a log, which is known as a hardy. To cut, place your tile over the hardy so the blade expresses the direction you want the break to go in.

5 Do not swing the hammer. Let it fall with its own weight onto the marble. The process is not as hazardous as it looks, although an occasional blood blister is probably inevitable. If you cut too heavily, the two blades will meet and blunt one another.

MICROMOSAIC

This requires immense patience, lots of practice and extremely fine cutting. Ensure that you have the sharpest cutters available, perhaps even reserving a pair to use only for micromosaic.

1 Tile cutters have two lugs to which the spring is attached. These determine the space between the blades and so prevent them from blunting. Micromosaic may require thinner pieces than this gap will allow you to cut. You can narrow the gap by filing down the lugs. When cutting from a large piece, start from the side.

2 Once it has become smaller, you have to put the tile cutters right over the top of it or your cut will not be accurate enough.

SMALTI

Smalti comes in different grades, the lowest of which looks a bit like recycled glass and is difficult to cut accurately. Most commercially available material should be of better quality, but if you have problems making fine cuts, then try cutting from the top rather than the side.

Smalti can be cut either with a hammer and hardy or with tile cutters. Tile cutters are more practical as you don't have to keep moving between your workbench and the place where the hardy is set up. The fragments created are needle-sharp and dangerous. Clear away the glass dust with a brush, not with your fingers.

GLAZED CERAMIC TILES

When cutting across the whole of a ceramic tile, you may find that the cut tends to curve. If this is a problem, you could use a tile cutting machine. The curves do have their own charm though. If a material has a particular characteristic it is often rewarding to use it. Think about designing a mosaic based on curved pieces.

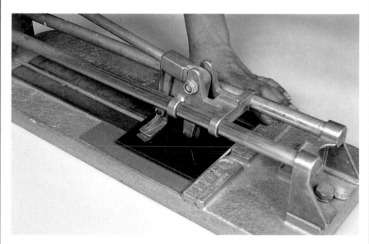

1 Although glazed ceramic tiles can be cut with tile cutters, it is sometimes useful to cut a tile down to a more manageable size using a large tile cutting machine, as shown here, or with the score-and-snap tile cutters available in most hardware stores. The principle is the same for both tools. First, score the tile.

2 Keeping the tile centered on the line you wish to break, gently but firmly press the handle. It will take some practice to get the feel of the pressure you need, but using up broken tiles should not be much of a problem to a mosaicist.

Design Techniques

This section describes the processes involved in producing a design and working from a drawing (for the processes involved in making this item, see Adhesive Techniques). Producing a working drawing is helpful in all mosaic-making.

Designing helps you to iron out any potential difficulties, and allows you to estimate the quantity of materials you require, so you can calculate the cost of the project. It is also essential if you plan to make a mosaic for someone else: when someone commissions a mosaic, they usually want to have an advance idea of what it is they are going to get.

It is not necessary when planning a design to work out how to lay it tile for tile. It would make the process an act of copying and probably take all the pleasure out of it. It is useful to produce a working drawing though. You may find yourself adapting it as you go along. Don't be alarmed by this; you need to be able to respond to the demands of the material. This section explains how to produce a drawing you can work from creatively.

YOU WILL NEED
Tools
Ruler
Pencil
Charcoal
Crayons

Materials
Layout paper
Brown paper
Water-soluble white craft glue
A selection of mosaic tiles

☞
Adhesive techniques, pages 50–51
Backgrounds, pages 54–55

WORKING FROM A DRAWING

1 Draw your design on layout paper. Because this paper is translucent, if you need to make amendments you can simply copy from a drawing placed beneath a fresh sheet. Do not be frightened of making your drawing bold and graphic.

Simplicity and stylization work well in mosaic. The fractured nature of the tiles and grout within any mosaic image means that there is always plenty going on, even in the simplest design.

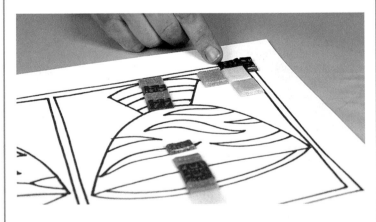

2 Select a palette of colors. In this design, the aim is to keep the bright, lively bowls in the foreground, setting them against a subtle background. It would be possible to contrast the foreground and background treatments by laying the bowls against a single color, but that would not create any tension between the two areas, and the bowls would be the only point of interest. Do not to treat the background as an afterthought (see Backgrounds).

3 |Match your colored pencils to the colors of the tiles you have selected. Try to make accurate matches.

4 |Draw the design using colored pencils, matching not only the colors but also their degrees of intensity. This can give you an idea of how well the design balances. If you feel your selection gives too much weight to one area of the composition, introduce another intense area to balance it. Balance, however, does not have to mean perfect symmetry—it can be achieved through detail, pattern, or complexity, as well as color.

5 |Make a tracing from your completed drawing so that you can reverse the design. It may seem like a minor point, but it is worth doing. Even if a design works at first, it may not be as effective when reversed. It is helpful to keep copies of your original drawings and tracings for future reference. Larger tracings, using sub-divisions, can also serve as fixing diagrams or key drawings (see Taking Templates).

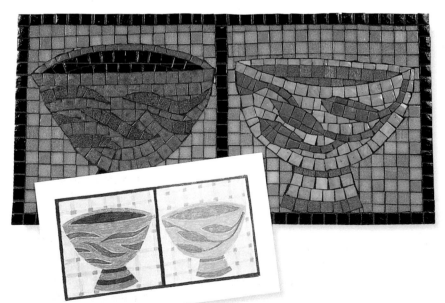

6 |Draw the reversed drawing on brown paper. It is always better to work on the matte side of the paper, which provides a slightly more absorbent surface for the glue.

▼ It is interesting to compare the sketch with the finished mosaic. Here, the background is not entirely accurate—the tonal contrast between foreground and background is slightly murkier in reality than in the drawing—but it is pretty true to the completed piece.

WORKING FROM A SOURCE OF INSPIRATION

Once you are aware of the visual qualities of objects around you, all sorts of unusual objects can provide inspiration. Some things are stimulating because of their color, some because of the composition, some because of their form. Making mosaics trains your eye to look in a new kind of way. The more you do, the more inspiration you will find.

YOU WILL NEED

Tools
Ruler
Pencil
Charcoal
Crayons

Materials
Layout paper
Brown paper
Water-soluble white craft
    glue
A selection of mosaic tiles

☞
**Design sources,
pages 14–17
Taking templates,
pages 122–125**

1 This mosaic is inspired by an old piece of polystyrene that was used to pack melons. It has a rhythm and a simplicity that works well as an abstract form, and it makes you think about light and shade. A pleasing pattern is created by slightly displacing a repeated form.

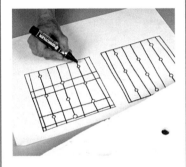

2 Decide on the size of the finished piece, and produce a scale drawing, working out the essential elements of the design.

3 Having decided on a basic structure for the design, you may want to play around with alternative ways of treating it. Running through your design options on paper in advance is quicker than doing so when you are making the mosaic. It is worth taking time at this stage to check you have made the right color and compositional choices.

5 By coloring a drawing accurately, you can spot any potential problems. You may be able to avoid the colors being too insipid or too strident. If you think your choice of tiles is not working well, reselect and redraw.

4 Make a selection of colors for your design. Try to find a pencil as close in color as possible to the mosaic tile you wish to use. It is worth investing in a selection of crayons that represent the color range of tiles you use.

6 Once you are confident the design is working, draw it onto your board. Charcoal is useful for this, because it is easy to rub off and redraw.

7 Cut the tiles as you go along, and build up the design area by area. This piece is not going to be grouted, so the tiles have been laid closer than they otherwise would have been. Ungrouted mosaic has a light, flickery effect and tends to look less flat than a grouted piece.

▼ With the mosaic completed, it is interesting to see how the source of inspiration relates to the finished item.

Direct Method

The direct method is a good technique for beginners, because it is relatively quick and easy. Its biggest advantage is that what you see while you are working is very close in appearance to the finished product.

The fact that as you work you can see the "right" side of the tiles is important when you are using marble, which can differ dramatically in tone, finish, and color from one side to another. It is also important with small and intricate mosaics, which depend on precise tonal gradation. It is also particularly suitable for pieces that employ texture or relief, because the indirect method tends to flatten out these effects. However, if you are working with glass or unglazed ceramic, which are the same color throughout, you can predict the appearance of the finished face from the back and can therefore use the indirect method.

YOU WILL NEED
Tools
Tile nippers
Adhesive brush
Paintbrush

Materials
Framed board
Charcoal
Building silicone
Mirror
White craft glue
Selections of tiles, including marble cubes and smalti
Paint

☞
Cutting techniques, pages 66–69
Finishing and fixing, pages 84–85

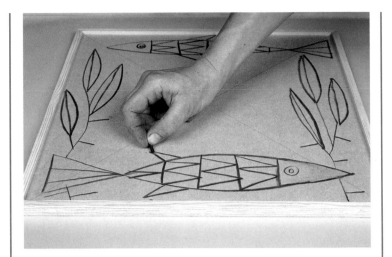

1 Cut a backing board for your mosaic mirror, and attach a frame around the edge of it. Rule lines between the opposing corners to identify the center of the board. Draw your design onto the board with charcoal, leaving the area for the mirror clear.

2 Spread building silicone on the center of the board. At this stage there is no need to get a smooth coat of glue over all the area the mirror will cover, just enough glue in the central area to hold the mirror once it is help upright.

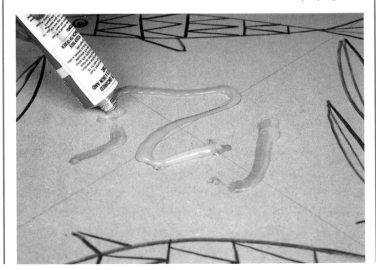

3 | Place the mirror, reflective side up, on the board. Move it around to spread the adhesive until it feels as if it is thoroughly and evenly coated. Use the diagonal rule lines as a guide for placement: they should meet each corner of the mirror. Press flat.

4 | Cut your tiles (see Cutting Techniques). This mirror frame is made with riven marble cut from cubes. Place glue on the board, not on the tiles. If you apply the glue too thickly it will squeeze up between the pieces. If it is too thin, the pieces will fall off. Begin by working on the principal features.

5 | The lines drawn represent changes in color of the material. As you begin work, you may find that the material has cut in an interesting or unpredictable way and you may want to amend your design accordingly. You would be unable to do this if the background were already laid.

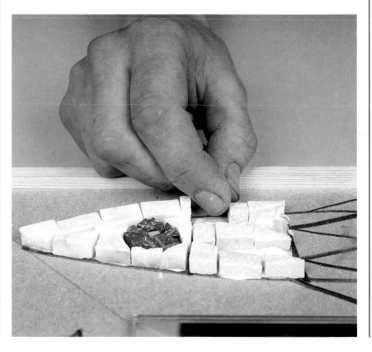

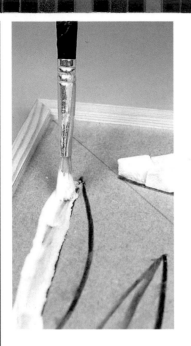

6 For each area of color, spread the craft glue within the charcoal lines using a small brush. By working on one area at a time you can keep to your design more accurately than if you were to spread adhesive over the whole board. It also allows you to work at your own pace.

7 If you have very tiny or narrow pieces to lay, it is helpful to put some adjacent larger tiles in place to support the smaller ones. Otherwise, unsupported tiles may fall over, into the glue.

8 Once the principal motifs have been laid, you can work on the background. If this is tricky to cut, like the gap between the leaves here, it may be useful to break a general rule and lay it at the same time as the foreground. If you do this before the glue has set, you can move tiles around, even opening the joints to redefine a shape slightly if you have an area that seems impossible to cut effectively.

9 | Continue putting in the background, still applying the craft glue to one small area at a time. This allows you to cut small batches of tesserae as you go along, rather than cutting too few or too many.

10 | In order to produce a neatly finished edge, work from the frame towards the fish motifs. When the glue is completely dry, paint the frame and when the paint is also dry screw mounts into the board so you can hang it up.

▲ This riven marble mirror uses the broken crystalline face of the marble to produce a textured surface that is left ungrouted.

Direct Method on Mesh

Mesh is useful for small domestic projects when you wish to have an idea of the finished effect as you work. This technique eliminates the need to work in the indirect method and simplifies the fixing process.

This technique also allows you to assemble the piece away from the actual location where you want to fix it. But you cannot use this technique for pieces which are to go outside, as the craft glue is not suitable for exterior use.

YOU WILL NEED

Tools	Materials
Scissors	Mesh
Permanent marker	Plastic wrap
Sticky tape	Water-soluble white craft
Tile nippers	glue
$\frac{1}{8}$in notched trowel	Selection of vitreous glass
Small board	tiles
Hammer	Cement-based adhesive
Grouting squeegee	Grout
Sponge	
Lint-free cloth	

☞
Direct method, pages 74–77 Outdoor direct adhesive method, pages 112–113

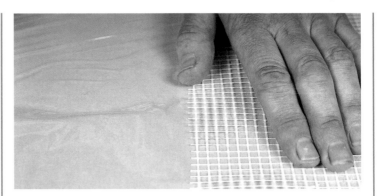

1 Cut the mesh carefully with scissors, so that you can use its straight lines as a grid for your design. Place a layer of plastic wrap or silicone-backed paper under the mesh, to prevent the piece sticking to the work surface.

Using a permanent marker, draw your design onto the mesh. Leave a margin of mesh at the edge.

2 To hold the mesh still while you work, tape down the edges. To liven up a muted design, this mosaic has a bright border. Cut tiles along an edge look unsightly, so start by laying the border with whole tiles. Apply the craft glue thickly to the mesh to hold the tiles firmly in position, since the mesh will flex as the mosaic is fixed in place.

3 Build up the design area by area. Do not apply too much glue at any one time, particularly in places that require intricate, time-consuming cutting of the tiles. If the glue is allowed to dry, it will leave a lumpy base for the tiles. Once the mosaic is complete, leave it to dry.

4 Once the whole mosaic is dry, remove the sticky tape and cut off the surplus mesh as closely to the tiles as you can. Remove the plastic wrap or paper from the back of the mosaic. After mixing cement-based adhesive with water to a creamy consistency, apply it evenly to the chosen surface, pressing down hard with a $1/8$in notched trowel.

6 In this case, the mid-tone of the mosaic is a slightly darker color than gray grout. A good tonal match has been achieved by mixing powders of gray and black grout. Mix powdered grout with water.

7 Apply grout to the mosaic and press into all the joints with a grouting squeggee. Clean off the grout with a moist sponge. Once the mosaic is dry, buff with a lint-free cloth.

5 Place the mosaic into the adhesive, carefully aligning the corners.

To guarantee the mosaic is bedded flat, take a hammer and small board and tap the entire surface. Leave to set.

▲ This panel uses selective cutting of tiles to contrast the shapes of the blocks of color with the overall strong rhythm of Opus Regulatum (see p. 106).

Double Reverse Method

This method allows you to lay the mosaic out as if you were working directly, then turn it over and gain the benefits of working in reverse as in the indirect method.

When you can't fix directly to a board or surface, but you are working with a material, such as glazed tiles or marble, which may have an entirely different appearance on one side from the other, you need a reverse method that allows you to see what the design is going to look like. This is when the double reverse method is helpful. You can only use this method if the tiles are roughly the same thickness. It is slightly trickier than simply working in reverse.

This tabletop is made from polished marble. The unfinished, sawn face of the material is dull, and its muted tones do not demonstrate the lively color of the finished side. This is why the double reverse method must be used.

YOU WILL NEED
Tools
Jigsaw
Compass
Pencil
Scissors
Charcoal
Paintbrush
2 large boards
Sponge
Grouting squeegee
Spatula or small tool
1/8 in notched trowel
Small board
Hammer
Lint-free cloth

Materials
Plywood or particleboard
Paper
Water-soluble white craft
   glue
Selection of marble tiles
Grout
Cement-based adhesive
Adhesive latex admix
Copper strip
Brass pins

1 Cut a circular board from a sheet of plywood or particleboard to use as a tabletop. On a piece of paper, draw two identical circles with a compass. Make them both fractionally smaller than the tabletop. Cut them out and make sure they fit neatly on the tabletop. Set one of the paper circles aside.

☞
**Indirect method,
pages 92–95
Grouting, pages 88–91**

2 When you are designing a mosaic you should always take into account the size of the tiles. An arrangement of tiles in a pattern like this needs to be planned carefully to ensure that it works out exactly. It can help to draw guidelines onto the paper using charcoal.

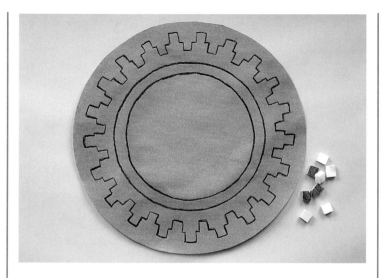

5 | Place the second paper circle on a flat surface. With a large paintbrush, coat the paper thoroughly with a stronger solution of glue (40% water and 60% white craft glue). It is vital that the paper is covered completely: any gaps will cause the mosaic to fall apart. Work quickly so the paper does not have time to stretch.

3 | When you are sure your design repeats correctly, sketch it onto the paper so you can follow it closely.

6 | Place the glue-coated paper on top of the mosaic. The circle should fit precisely. If it does not, realign it until you have a perfect fit. Press the paper flat on the polished face of the tiles.

4 | Using a weak mix of water-soluble white craft glue (70% water and 30% glue), stick the marble tiles to the paper. Make sure you get the spacing right, because this is how the completed mosaic will appear. Begin with the border and, when it is completed, fill in the center. Once finished, set aside to dry.

7 | Moving quickly, sandwich the mosaic between two boards, gripping both tightly, and turn it over. Remove the upper board. Press the mosaic hard through the paper to ensure every piece has made contact with the glue-coated paper now on the bottom. Leave to dry.

9 | Pregrout the mosaic (see Grouting). Clean the grout off with a sponge that has been thoroughly squeezed dry.

8 | Wet the top paper thoroughly with a moist but not dripping wet sponge. Leave it for ten minutes, checking regularly to see if any paler patches have appeared. If so, rewet thoroughly, but do not use so much water that it soaks into the paper underneath. After ten minutes the paper should be saturated and will have turned a dark brown. Experiment with peeling back the paper. If there is some resistance, rewet. If not peel it back, starting from one corner and peeling toward the center. Place the paper back down again (it will not restick) and peel from the opposite side. If you displace any tiles in the process of peeling, put them back into the hole they came from, checking the joint is correctly aligned. Reglue any tiles that have come loose. Leave to dry.

10 | Once the grout is in the joints and the mosaic is clean, you can compensate for any slight differences in the depth of the tiles by laying a coat of cement-based adhesive up to the thickness of the thickest tile. This is known as "buttering the back." Apply it with a spatula or small tool, and make sure it is level.

11 Mix the cement-based adhesive with a latex admix combined with water so that it bonds securely with the wood. Use a ⅛in notched trowel to apply adhesive to the tabletop. The trowel acts as a gauge to ensure the adhesive is applied evenly, so make sure you press hard.

Put your mosaic on a large board. If the mosaic is small enough, place the tabletop on it, rather than turning the wet, heavy mosaic over. Turn over (see Indirect Method).

13 Wet the paper thoroughly; when saturated, peel it off. While the adhesive is still wet, carefully sponge any remaining glue and grout from the surface. Work from the edge to the center so you do not move any tiles. The aim is not to clean the surface, but rather to ensure the grout is smooth. Leave to dry. Regrout from the front. Clean off with a sponge. Buff up with a lint-free cloth.

14 Once the mosaic is dry, attach a copper strip to the outside of the board to act as a frame. Use brass pins to attach the strip, because these will not rust. Finally, grout the junction between the mosaic and the frame.

12 To ensure the surface is flat and there is no air trapped between the layers of adhesive, place a small board on top of the mosaic and move it across, gently tapping it with a hammer. The aim is to make the thicker tiles butt up close to the board, displacing adhesive, which then will support the thinner ones. This creates an even, flat surface.

▶ The finished tabletop uses the subtle tones of marble to bring warmth to a geometric pattern.

Finishing and Fixing

The overall impression of a mosaic can be spoiled if the work is not finished to a high standard. These details make a mosaic complete and presentable. Although such finishing touches may seem minor, it is surprising how much some small details can affect the final impression of a piece.

It is easy to think that once a mosaic is grouted or the tiles fixed into place, that you have finished your work. After laboring away making a piece, sometimes for weeks, it seems only fair to think of it as finished when you have it stuck in position. There are, however, minor details in presentation that can make all the difference to how it looks.

Finishing and fixing are not only matters of presentation; they are essential for protecting your mosaic from the elements and accidental damage. Presented here are some of the most common finishing processes which may apply to your mosaic.

☞
**Casting, pages 58–61
Three-dimensional
surfaces, pages 128–129
Indirect method,
pages 92–95
Outdoor direct method,
pages 112–113**

▲ Applying sealant to a cast slab. Polished marble gains some chemical resistance to staining from the structure of its glassy surface, but honed or riven marble is more vulnerable and needs protection. To give terra-cotta and marble some protection from dirt and grime, apply sealant with a lint-free cloth. If you have made a tabletop with marble tiles, it is a good idea to use a sealant that also protects it against staining from spillages of oil and wine.

▲ Buff up a completed mosaic with a dry cloth. It is surprising how easy it is not to clean a mosaic properly. Sometimes it is difficult to see whether or not all the grout has been removed, particularly when the tiles are dark in color. The cloth abrades any film of grout left on the surface, and leaves the mosaic shiny and clean. The only exception to this is unglazed ceramic, which must be cleaned with water during the fixing process, because it will not rub clean later on.

◄ Paint the frames and backs of completed mosaics. It is more sensible to do this before the mosaic is fixed, although you will probably need to retouch the paint once the mosaic is in position. Give as much thought to the paint color as you gave to the color of the tiles, because it will be setting off the appearance of the completed work.

▲ Be careful framing tabletops. The frame must not extend higher than the level of the fixed mosaic or it will catch against things you place on the table. If the frame is made for a table which you plan to use outside this is even more critical, since a lip that extends higher than the level of the tiles will act as a water trap.

▲ Tile trim should be carefully applied. This piece of tile trim demonstrates the way in which tesserae should fit neatly flush up to the edge, protecting what would otherwise be vulnerable tiles. The tile trim should be feathered in to the adhesive (gradually building up to the trim with adhesive) to avoid an unsightly bump in a row of tiles, created by the thickness of the trim beneath.

▼ Pay attention to the ways in which you attach fixings to the completed mosaic. Measure carefully to ensure that they are placed at an even distance from each side of the piece. If they are unevenly placed, it will be difficult to get the piece to hang straight.

▼ Use eyelet screws for hanging mosaics on walls. Fix two at even intervals to the back of the mosaic, then lace brass wire through the rings.

▲ When cleaning mirrors incorporated in a mosaic, avoid spraying glass cleaner on the mosaic itself. If the grout absorbs the cleaner, it may change color slightly, giving it a blotchy appearance.

Glass and Silicone

Stained glass and mosaic are similar in many ways. Both materials fracture an image through a series of joints. These materials can be used together to good effect and the combination of vitreous glass mosaic tiles and stained glass gives a very striking result.

Although stained glass needs light for the full effect of the color to be appreciated, the use of opaque glass and the mosaic technique means that this lampshade is also appealing when it is not illuminated. This does mean giving some thought to the way the colors work together. Mirror glass can provide an additional reflective element, which also helps to throw light around when the lamp is switched on.

YOU WILL NEED
Tools
Glass cutter
Tile nippers

Materials
Stained glass tiles
Vitreous glass tiles
Table lamp
Lampshade
Building silicone or glass
    glue
Copper wire
Self-adhesive copper tape
Copper rings

☞
**Cutting techniques,
pages 66–69
Finishing and fixing,
pages 84–85**

1 Choose stained glass and vitreous glass tiles that complement each other. Remove the existing paper shade from its substructure, from which you will hang your mosaic strips. After calculating the length of the glass pieces, bearing in mind that the copper wire and rings by which they are hung will increase their length, cut glass strips.

2 To make stained glass mosaic tiles, cut additional glass strips with the glass cutter. These narrow strips of glass are easy to cut into square tiles with normal tile nippers.

3 Apply clear building silicone or glass glue to the glass strips. Do not apply so much that it squeezes up between the joints.

8 When the substructure is covered in tape and the rings are attached, hook the mosaic strips to the copper rings. Make sure you have an equal number on both sides of the shade. The glass shade is attached to the lamp as you would a normal shade.

4 Place the tiles you cut into the building silicone. This piece will not be grouted, so take care to keep surfaces clean and the spacing even.

6 Thread the copper rings onto the base of the shade before you apply the copper tape, or the process of threading them may damage it.

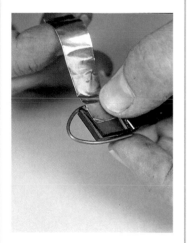

7 Copper tape can be used to cover the shade's substructure. It is best to cut the tape into small pieces and apply each piece individually.

5 The glass strips will be attached to the lampshade with hooks made of copper wire. These are simple to make: just bend a small piece of copper wire over the top of the strip and tape it into position with self-adhesive copper tape.

▲ Turn on the lamp and appreciate how the light shines through the glass.

Grouting

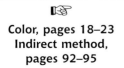

Grout is the matrix that goes between the tiles. It has a major influence on the finished appearance of the mosaic, so although the application of grout is the final stage of fixing a mosaic, it must not be treated as an after-thought.

A mosaic changes dramatically when it is grouted. Grout unites the mosaic and draws attention to the way it has been laid. It also affects the way the colors work together, because colors relate to one another in the mosaic with grout as an intervening medium (see Color for more on the ways grout alters the appearance of a finished mosaic).

It is possible to buy ready-mixed grout, but it is generally cheaper and better to work with in its powdered form. Grout is commonly available in three shades: white, gray, and black. Unless you are deliberately seeking a contrast, it is best to select the one that matches the principal tone of the mosaic: if it is mostly dark, choose black grout; for mid-tones, use gray; and for pale items, choose white. It is possible to match the color of the mosaic by adding dry admixes of colorant to white grout. However, this disguises the mosaic effect. If you do choose to use colorant, it is essential to make a note of the ratio of admix to grout powder in order to reproduce the shade for a later batch.

When you tile a wall or floor, you set the tiles with adhesive and grout them later. If the adhesive squeezes up between the joints, tilers use a special tool to scrape out the excess. This is not the way it works with mosaic. Tesserae are generally very thin. If you place them directly into adhesive, even if it has only been thinly applied, the adhesive will squeeze up between the joints.

However, the joints in mosaics are of a different character to those with tiles: because there are hundreds of them, all going off in different directions, it is impossible to scrape them out. The only way to overcome this

☞
Color, pages 18–23
Indirect method,
pages 92–95

problem is to pregrout. By applying the grout to the back of the paper on which the mosaic is stuck, you create a barrier that prevents unwanted adhesive from squeezing up between the tiles. Later, once the mosaic has been set, you grout again from the front.

When your mosaic is complete, it is ready to be grouted. Grouting a piece which has been fixed with the direct method (see pages 74–77) is merely a matter of pushing the grout into the joints and cleaning off with a sponge. This section explains the more complex process by which you grout pieces made by the indirect method (see pages 92–95).

YOU WILL NEED

Tools	Materials
Container for grout	1 sheet mosaic tiles
Container for water	Grout
Container for adhesive	Cement-based adhesive
2 wallpaper scrapers, one for mixing grout, one for adhesive	Board
Grouting squeegee	
Sponge	
Notched trowel	

1 Put the powdered grout into a container. It is important to make up a large enough batch, because once you begin, you need to work quickly. The paper will be absorbing water from the grout you have applied, and you must turn the mosaic over before the bond between tile and paper is affected by moisture.

2 | Mix the grout with water to a creamy consistency. Do not make the mix too wet.
Fill a second container with water, which you will use when you sponge off the excess grout. Mix up your adhesive.

3 | Apply the grout to the back of the tiles with a grouting squeegee. Make sure all the joints are filled. This is most easily achieved by sweeping the squeegee horizontally and then vertically.

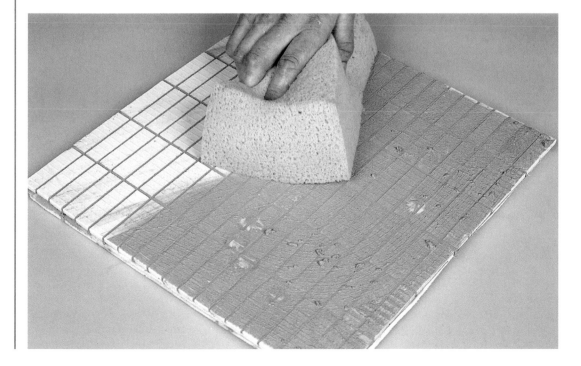

4 | Wet your sponge and squeeze it out as much as possible. Clean off the excess grout by pressing one side of the sponge flat to the mosaic. Turn the sponge over and repeat. It is essential to use a clean area of sponge each time: otherwise you will simply reapply all the grout you previously removed. Once clean, set aside.

5 | Apply adhesive to the board, using a notched trowel.

7 | Wipe the paper with a damp sponge. Do not make it so wet that water runs into the adhesive.

6 | Pick up your sheet of mosaic and turn it over. The easiest way to do this is by holding either two corners or two opposing edges of the paper and pulling outward slightly as you might pull a sheet. Do not put one hand underneath and the other on top because the paper might flop or fold, causing tiles to fall off. Place the mosaic into the adhesive with the backing paper face-up. Make sure you align it correctly, with nothing overhanging the board.

8 | When the paper is really dark in color (it generally takes about ten minutes) peel it off. Start from one corner and peel toward the center. Place the paper back down again (it will not restick) and peel from the opposite side. If you displace any tiles in the process of peeling, put them back into the hole they came from, checking the joint is correctly aligned. Once again, clean the mosaic with a sponge that has been thoroughly squeezed out. This will ensure that the grout is smooth and free from lumps. Leave to dry.

9 | Regrout from the front. Because the mosaic has set, you can be more vigorous.

10 | Sponge the grout off the face of the mosaic, as before. When it has dried, buff up with a lint-free cloth.

▲ Mosaic can be used to create calming effects—not every mosaic has to have bright colors and patterns. This panel, destined for use in a modern kitchen, will not fight for your attention but gives an interesting background texture.

Indirect Method on Paper

The indirect method is sometimes also known as the reverse method, because the image has to be reversed, and it is the method most commonly used by professional mosaicists. The advantage of this method is that the mosaic can be made away from the place in which it is finally fixed.

In this technique the mosaic is constructed onto paper, and not directly onto its final surface. The paper is a temporary surface, and the mosaic is fixed the right way up when it is finally positioned in its permanent location.

In order to work this way it is necessary to reverse any drawing you make. This is relatively easy. You can either trace the drawing, or use a lightbox. You can even draw the image on the back of the paper with a thick permanent marker, because the pen will go through the paper and produce an instant reversal of the drawing.

☞
Grouting, pages 88–91
Opus, pages 106–107

1 Cut a piece of brown paper slightly smaller than the size of the board to which you plan to fix the mosaic. Draw out your design onto the matte side of the paper. Remember that any drawing you do will be reversed in the final mosaic, so numbers and letters need to be drawn in reverse at this stage.

YOU WILL NEED
Tools
Scissors
Board
Adhesive brush
Tile nippers
Grouting squeegee
Sponge
1/8in notched trowel

Materials
Brown paper
Permanent marker
Water-soluble white craft
  glue
Tiles, here vitreous glass
  mosaic tiles
Grout
Cement-based adhesive

3 The glue needs to dry out thoroughly when you have all the tiles in place. Once dry, pregrout the mosaic (see Grouting), pushing the grout into the joints with a grouting squeegee.

2 Stick the mosaic to the paper using a water-soluble white craft glue diluted 50:50 with water. Start the piece by laying the border with whole tiles, using the adhesive brush to apply glue to the paper as you work. When the border is in place, lay the main motif, and fill in the background last (see Opus).

4 Use a damp sponge to remove excess grout from the back of the tiles. Grout must not be left on the back of the mosaic because it will prevent proper bonding with the adhesive on the board.

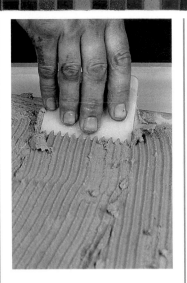

5 Mix up cement-based adhesive (see Adhesives) and use a 1/8in notched trowel to apply a layer to the board. Make sure the teeth of the trowel touch the board, to ensure that an even thickness of adhesive is laid across the whole area.

7 Wet the paper with a thoroughly wet sponge. Leave the paper to absorb moisture for at least five to ten minutes.

6 Place the pregrouted mosaic into the adhesive, paper side up. Be sure to align the corners properly before putting the paper in place.

8 Peel off the paper starting from one corner and working towards the center. The tiles along the edge of the mosaic are always the most vulnerable to movement. If any come away, place them back in position ensuring there is adequate adhesive behind them. Once you have peeled into the center of the mosaic, replace the paper (it will not restick) and start to peel from the opposing corner. Once the paper has been peeled off, clean the mosaic immediately with a thoroughly squeezed out sponge. Leave to dry.

9 Once the mosaic is dry, regrout from the front, making sure that all the tiny holes are filled.

10 Wet a clean sponge and squeeze out as much water as possible. Use this to clean the grout off the mosaic and buff up with a soft cloth.

▲ The finished piece has a smooth surface, as a result of using the indirect method. It was assembled in comfort at a workbench before being fixed into place.

Indirect Method with Plastic

You cannot use the indirect method on glazed tiles, because it is impossible to plan a design in terms of color and pattern without seeing what you are creating. However with small projects, such as this tile-sized piece, you can use a variant of the indirect method by arranging the design the right way up and sticking plastic to the face.

This method is not to be used for large pieces, as there is too much risk of the tiles moving around as you lay on the adhesive-backed plastic. It is important to keep your working surface clean as dust may interfere with adhesion of the plastic to the tiles. An advantage to this method is that even if you use tiles of different thicknesses the finished piece will have a flat surface.

YOU WILL NEED

Tools
Scissors
Tile nippers
Notched trowel
Hammer
Rubber gloves
Grouting squeegee
Sponge
Lint-free cloth

Materials
2 boards
Adhesive-backed plastic
Glazed ceramic tiles
Cement-based adhesive
Latex admix
Grout

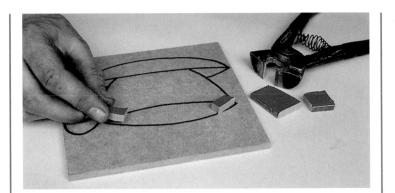

1 Draw your design on a board or sheet of paper. Decide on the colors you wish to use. Cut a piece of adhesive-backed plastic to the size of your design and set aside.

2 Dry lay (lay the tiles without glue) on the board or paper.

☞
Cutting techniques, pages 66–69
Grouting, pages 88–91

3 Once the design is complete, peel the adhesive-backed plastic from its backing and lay it on the face of the tiles. Be careful not to disturb the tiles, because once they have adhered to the plastic, you cannot change their positions.

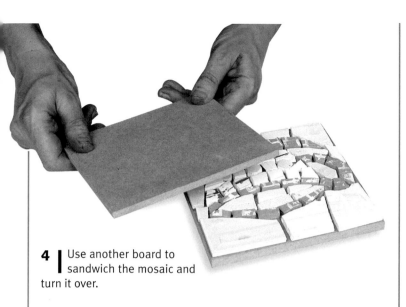

4 | Use another board to sandwich the mosaic and turn it over.

5 | Mix up the cement-based adhesive. This adhesive requires a latex admix combined with water to bond securely to wood. This is usually mixed in a 50:50 ratio, but check the manufacturer's instructions. Using the notches on the trowel to make sure you spread an even quantity across the whole area, trowel the mixture onto the surface on which the mosaic is going to be placed. The mosaic is not pregrouted in this method.

Lay the tile-sized mosaic into the adhesive, aligning the corners carefully.

6 | With a small board and hammer, beat the mosaic flat to ensure that even the smallest piece has made contact with the adhesive.

7 | Because you have not pregrouted, there is no need to peel the plastic off immediately. Give the adhesive time to dry before attempting to peel away the plastic.

8 | Mix powdered grout and water to a fairly stiff consistency. If the grout is firm, it is less likely that you will have to grout again; with a wet mix, water evaporates from the joints, causing them to sink. You can grout a small item like this with your hands, rather than using a squeegee, as long as you wear rubber gloves. Sponge clean, then leave to dry. Buff with a lint-free cloth.

▼ This technique is ideal for small panels such as this one, which is themed for an area of tiling in a kitchen.

Laying Tesserae

The way in which tiles are laid expresses a mood or gives a sense of animation or calm to a mosaic. This section looks at some of the ways in which they can be laid. It also shows you some of the methods by which you can make the grout lines flow as smoothly as possible.

When we talk about laying mosaic, what we are really discussing are different ways of arranging the space between mosaic tiles. It doesn't really matter how far apart you space the tiles from one another, but whatever you decide the gap is going to be, you must maintain it for the whole of your mosaic. There may be a creative way of spacing the tiles so that there is a contrasting gap size in different areas or motifs, but as a general rule, a mosaic will look much more harmonious if the spacing is even.

QUARTER TILES

Most mosaicists work with quarter tiles as a balance between using tesserae which are small enough to make detailed designs, but not having to make too many cuts.

☞
Andamenti, pages 52–53
Opus, pages 104–111

▲ This way of arranging tiles is known as Opus Regulatum. It is mosaic which is laid straight in two directions. It is the way mosaic tiles are laid when supplied from the factory.

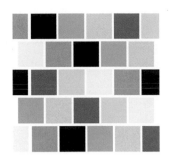

▲ This is also known as Opus Regulatum or Opus Tessalatum. The rows are offset, and it is important to try and maintain the keying effect, since the eye is quick to notice areas of geometrical regularity.

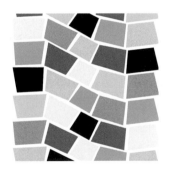

▲ This is Opus Regulatum which has been laid to express movement. In order to allow the tiles to flow around curves they have been slightly angled along one side. It always looks best if the angles are kept flowing in the same direction.

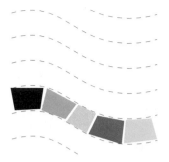

▲ This diagram demonstrates an undesirable way to lay mosaic. One angle has been cut to help the tiles move around a curve, but another angled piece has been cut as an answering shape. If you find yourself cutting angles on a tile opposite to the ones you cut on the previous tile, you need not have cut the first angle.

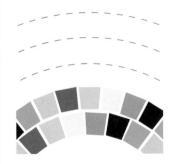

▲ This diagram shows how the tiles should be laid to make the most flowing curves. The angles of the cuts express the direction in which the curve is traveling. Each tile is cut evenly on both sides, so it tapers toward the base. Compare this to the next diagram where the tiles are cut in both directions.

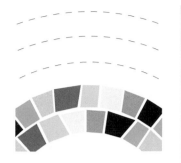

▲ This shows the effect of cuts which do not echo the direction of the curve. It is distracting to the eye and interferes with the rhythm of the curves.

▲ To make tiles radiate out from a central point you will have to cut tiles on both sides.

▲ Once you have produced a slightly odd cut, the next tiles

are forced into increasingly odd angles by it. Discard any oddly cut tiles and start again.

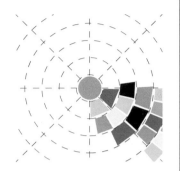

▲ If you are working in this radiating way and are finding it hard to make angled cuts which express the way the tiles move round the circle, you may find it helpful to divide up the space geometrically with a ruler. Geometrical precision is not necessary, but if you place the tile you plan to cut over the marks you have made on the paper they remind you which side of the tile you have to cut.

▲ You can create emphasis by laying sections of mosaic in opposing directions.

▲ This is an example of Opus Circumactum. Where the tops of the circles meet and the area of infill begins it is important that you cut the tiles equally on all sides so no circle is given precedence over another.

▲ This fan design is a traditional mosaic background. To make it work effectively it is important to observe the previous remarks about cutting sympathetically to the flow of each curve.

HALF TILES

You can employ many of the same laying methods just as creatively by using half tiles instead of quarter tiles.

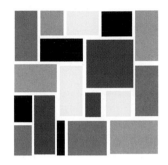

▲ This is a random mix of half, quarter and whole tiles. This sort of treatment was very popular in the 1950s, when contrast was of great interest to mosaicists.

▲ This is herringbone pattern, also known as Opus Spicatum. It creates quite a busy effect, and can be rather tricky to arrange around images.

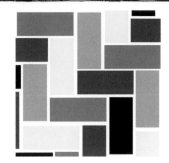

▲ This basketweave effect has an attractive rhythm and is quick to produce.

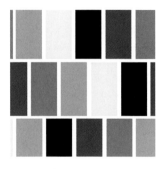

▲ This is a version of Opus Tessalatum for half tiles.

▲ The rules which apply to producing this design effectively in quarter tiles also apply here. Using half tiles does increase the speed at which you can work, and this pattern is quick to produce.

▲ This is a version of Opus Tessalatum moving around a curve. You could use half and quarter tiles in the same piece.

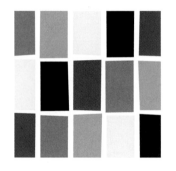

▲ Opus Regulatum with half tiles is saved from dullness by the variation in the cut edges.

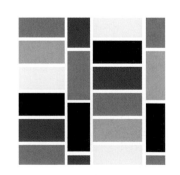

▲ Contrasting the directions in which tiles are laid creates strong lines in a background.

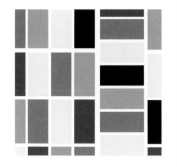

▲ You can break a repeating system by suddenly laying the tiles in a different direction. This background treatment is worth considering to give emphasis in particular parts of your mosaic.

TILES CUT TO SPECIAL SHAPES

Part of the enjoyment of making mosaic involves cutting the tiles. At first this can seem rather off-putting, but gradually you gain control of the tile nippers and they become as versatile as scissors, allowing you to cut ambitious and interesting shapes of tiles.

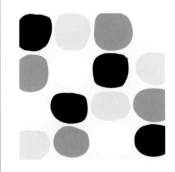

▲ Circles can be laid to set up their own patterns. A certain degree of wobbliness in the shape only adds to the charm.

▲ Randomly curved shapes were once very popular, and they do give a lovely organic, rather scaley impression.

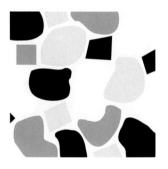

▲ To vary the effect of organic shapes, and to speed up the process, you can include some quarter tiles. It can be useful to combine different shapes, as you are often left with some strange-shaped spaces when cutting and laying these tiles.

▲ This version of Opus Palladianum gives a lively, fractured effect.

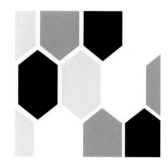

▲ These honeycomb shapes are rather arduous to cut, but give a wonderful pattern.

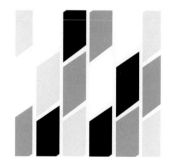

▲ Long two-angled cuts like these are useful as patterns in themselves, but they also help create a feathery impression.

A SINGLE SHAPE DESCRIBED IN A SERIES OF WAYS

This leaf shape has been made up in six different ways in order to drive home the point that the ways in which you can construct a single form are almost infinite. There is also no single right way to do it. Different ways of cutting and laying create a variety of impressions, and it is up to you to decide what is appropriate for the mosaic you are producing.

▲ The leaf here has been conventionally treated. Note that the bottom is laid slightly differently to the top. The single tile at the top is a very satisfactory leaf-tip, but the two cut tiles at the bottom do help to suggest a stem.

▲ This way of laying a leaf might be useful if you wanted to suggest movement.

▲ This arrangement makes a more obvious reference to a central stem.

▲ Providing you are disciplined about laying tiles precisely to the outside of the shape, this can be a quick way of forming a leaf.

▲ This suggests the symmetry and skeleton of a leaf. It is a pleasing effect, but would be difficult to achieve if the leaf were large, as it requires long cuts from a whole tile.

▲ This approach refers to a central stalk and also divides the shape skeletally.

Micromosaic

It is impossible to pretend that micromosaic is anything other than time-consuming and tricky. You have to be prepared for hours of patient labor, and because the image grows at a snail's pace, you do not get immediate gratification. However, micromosaic has a unique effect.

This project was taken on as a technical challenge and represents months of work. If you want to try working with micromosaic, it would be best to start with something really small. If you work with normal size tiles, you can experiment with fine transitions of color only if the whole piece is very large. If it is not possible to work large, the only other way you can experiment like that is to work with really small pieces. It also increases the scope of your mosaic palette, particularly in relation to tone. You can use the natural tonal variations within a piece of marble to create sophisticated effects.

YOU WILL NEED
Tools
As for indirect method, plus
tweezers and a pin

Materials
Brown paper
Gummed paper tape
Water-soluble white craft glue
Selection of marble rods

☞
Adhesive techniques, pages 50–51
Grouting, pages 88–91
Indirect method, pages 92–95

1 This micromosaic is a reproduction of the theater scene from the House of the Tragic Poet in Pompeii, Italy, an ancient Roman town that was buried by a volcanic eruption in AD79. Reproducing in accurate detail the lines of coursing of the original and the tonal and color variations represents a real challenge.

2 Because the piece aims to reproduce the original as accurately as possible, a sketch has been made exactly the same size as the original, delineating the principal features. The piece is being made by the indirect method (see p. 96), so the drawing must be reversed.

3 When working with such tiny pieces, the slightest degree of paper-stretching presents problems (see Common Mistakes). If the paper expands at all as the glue is applied, it can dislodge the tiny tesserae, creating gaps. In order to prevent this, the paper needs to be stretched before any tiles are stuck to it. Immerse the paper in water and stick it to the board with brown paper tape. Once the paper has dried, the design can be drawn onto it.

5 Thin rods of marble are cut and the individual tesserae are cut down from them. Enormous care needs to be taken in cutting these individual pieces since any swelling of the tiny cubes at the base or at the top means that adjoining tiles will not fit neatly against each other, leaving unsightly gaps. The tiny cubes therefore need to be cut absolutely straight.

6 The only way to work with such minute pieces is with a pair of tweezers and a pin. Spread glue over a very small area of paper at a time. Lay the defining outer lines first, leave them to dry, and then work up against them. Otherwise, it is easy to keep knocking the cubes out of position.

7 Some of the pieces in these faces are smaller than the head of a pin. The mosaic will probably need some reworking in the fixing process, because facial expressions are apt to change enormously with even tiny displacements in the position of a tile. Once the mosaic is complete, pre-grout it (see p. 89), build up any differences in levels by buttering the back (see p. 51), and fix in place (see Indirect Method, p. 92).

4 Here you can see the range of marble colors chosen to stand in for those used in the original. When working at such a scale, the tonal variation within a single cube can represent a considerable color change.

◄ You can see that the way the tiles are laid gives a variety of rhythmic effects to the finished piece. The way the sheepskin around the men's waists is laid will give an impression of the animal's shaggy coat. The way the musculature in the legs is laid helps describe the form. The principles behind working at this scale are the same as working a larger scale, just trickier to achieve.

Opus

The term Opus means "work" in Latin. The second part of each Opus name describes the style of laying, also based on Latin terminology. These terms are shorthand ways of describing the system by which the tiles in any mosaic are laid relative to one another.

Shown here are the traditional systems of building up your mosaic backgrounds. You can also make up your own ways of working, particularly if you want to make a distinctive feature of the laying or andamenti within your mosaic. Once you begin to take notice of the different types of Opus, you will appreciate how varied their effects on a mosaic's final appearance can be.

YOU WILL NEED
Tools
Scissors
Board
Tile nippers
Adhesive brush
Grouting squeegee
1/8in notched trowel
Sponge

Materials
Brown paper
Charcoal
Tiles
Water-soluble white craft
    glue
Grout
Cement-based adhesive

☞
Andamenti, pages 52–53
**Cutting techniques,
pages 66–69**
Laying, pages 98–101

OPUS PALLADIANUM

This kind of background treatment is lively and effective. It is also quick and easy to produce. It is an ideal way of working for a beginner, or someone who is still perfecting their cutting skills. You will produce a harmonious and balanced-looking background by leaving an even gap between tiles. The gap can be small or large, since in either case the size of the gap is less important than the fact that it is even throughout.

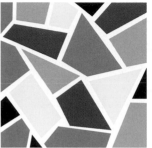

Opus Palladianum

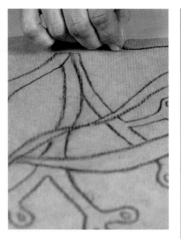

1 Draw your design onto the matte side of a piece of brown paper, cut fractionally smaller than the board to which you plan to fix the mosaic. Use charcoal as it allows for corrections to be made easily. As this small panel is going to have a practical function as a pot stand, it is a good idea to have a border of whole tiles around the outside, since small pieces are likely to get damaged.

2 Lay the whole tile border around the edge of the paper, using the craft glue diluted 50:50 with water. If you need to cut tiles in order to make the mosaic fit the paper, do not do so at the corners, as this might interfere with the balance of the piece.

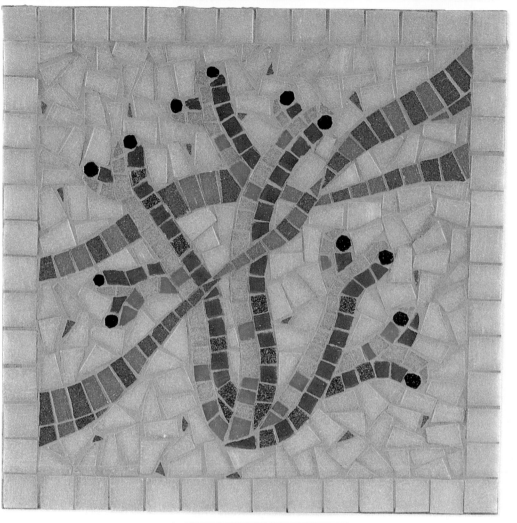

3 | Next, stick the most significant features before the background. The main features are the focus of the mosaic, and you do not want the background to dominate them. Here, the strips of weed are laid before the sea plant has been begun, even though the sea plant is clearly a more important item. This is because they appear in front of the plant, so they need to be glued in place first.

4 | Once the main features are complete you can lay the background. This kind of cutting is sometimes known as crazy-laid mosaic, since it is rather like crazy paving. The tiles are fractured haphazardly to start with, but as you get closer to the main features you will increasingly find yourself having to cut special shapes to fit the spaces left. The sophistication of the cutting will develop as you work. You may find it helpful to sketch the shape of the piece you need onto the tile you are planning to cut.

▲ The effect this technique gives is lively and free, making it particularly good for beginners.

5 | Build up the background area by area. There is no real need in the case of this technique to start in any particular place. You might wish, as here, to add in the odd tile of a contrasting color to connect the background with the foreground. When the mosaic is complete, fix it by following the instructions for the indirect method.

OPUS REGULATUM

This term refers to mosaic which has been straight-laid in one or two directions. An example of Opus Regulatum is sheeted-up mosaic tiles bought from the factory, which are straight-laid in both directions. It is possible to offset the rows so that they line up in only one direction, creating a sense of movement, and this kind of mosaic is also known as Opus Regulatum, or sometimes as Opus Tessalatum.

The appeal of mosaic laid in this way is that it is calming as a background. If the main features of your mosaic are lively and frantic, or the colors particularly bright, this background might be a good choice as a contrast. It is also useful to be able to make decorative features which fit into the sheeted-up material from the factory.

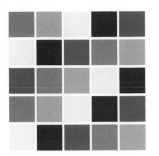

Opus Regulatum

Opus Tessalatum

YOU WILL NEED

Tools
Scissors
Board
Tile nippers
Adhesive brush
Grouting squeegee
Sponge
1/8in notched trowel

Materials
Brown paper
Permanent marker
Tiles
Water-soluble white craft glue
Grout
Cement-based adhesive

1 Draw your design on the matte side of a piece of brown paper, cut fractionally smaller than the board onto which you plan to fix it. Here the animated shape of the starfish is interesting enough to be able to withstand the rather static effect of straight-laying the tiles.

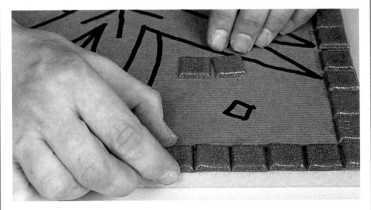

2 Lay a border or whole tiles around the sheet of paper first, using a water-soluble white craft glue diluted 50:50 with water. This is important as you want to be able to spread out or tighten the joints between the tiles as freely as possible to ensure you have to do as little cutting as possible. This whole-tile border protects the cut tiles on the inside of the mosaic.

3 Next, lay the principal features. When working to a sharp point like this it can be helpful to start from the point and work outward, so you can cut the first tile to the exact shape and size needed. Very small angled pieces of mosaic are vulnerable to movement in the fixing process.

4 Once the main features are in place you can lay the background. In order to make this background more interesting the pieces have been cut into quarters. It is important when working with a simple background that you work out how you are going to lay the tiles, so eliminating the need to cut them down further, particularly at the edges of the design, where they might look rather scrappy. Before you start to stick, space them out so you can be sure you finish on a whole tile. If they do not work out perfectly, rearrange them until they do.

5 Carry on laying the tiles until the background is complete. These tiles have been offset to give a little animation to what can be rather a static effect. Once the mosaic is complete, fix it by following the instructions for the indirect method.

▶ In the finished panel the starfish has wonderful impact in both color and form, which is accentuated by the calming effect of the background.

Opus Circumactum

OPUS CIRCUMACTUM

This technique is related to the traditional mosaic fan shape. It is useful for square mosaics, where the tiles are laid in quarter circles from the edge, and meet neatly in the center. The effect is rhythmic and pleasing.

It isn't always easy to select a background treatment for a mosaic, particularly a small one. Opus Regulatum can give a very static effect. Opus Vermiculatum can be rather frantic and chaotic. Opus Palladianum is very pleasing, but it is rather busy. Sometimes you need a background treatment which is interesting and gives a sense of movement, without being overbearing. Opus Circumactum is probably the best solution in this case.

YOU WILL NEED
Tools
Scissors
Board
Pair of compasses
Tile nippers
Adhesive brush
Grouting squeegee
1/8in notched trowel

Materials
Brown paper
Permanent marker
Tiles
Water-soluble white craft glue
Grout
Cement-based adhesive

1 Cut a piece of brown paper fractionally smaller than the board onto which you plan to fix your mosaic. Draw your design onto the matte side of the paper. As you plan to lay a series of circles coming in from the corners, it is a good idea to draw up the circles with a pair of compasses. You can draw the circles in freehand, but they are unlikely to be very accurate. Any irregularities will be taken up and expressed all the way across the mosaic.

2 Lay the border, sticking the tiles in place with water-soluble craft glue diluted 50:50 with water. If you need to cut tiles (see Cutting Techniques) in order to complete the border neatly, make sure you do not lay them at the corners as this can look cumbersome.

3 Next, lay the tiles which describe the predominant feature of your mosaic. In this case the mosaic depicts a pair of shells. Complete these before starting to lay the background.

4 Once the main image is complete, start laying the background. Start with the upper edge of one quarter circle. Work from the upper edge to the corner. You may find it helpful to sketch in further guide lines with the pair of compasses, as it is surprisingly easy to flatten out the circles or introduce inaccuracies where they abut the border and main motifs. Once one quarter circle is complete, move on to the next. These circles have been made slightly livelier by using a closely related but slightly different color of tile mixed into the background. When all four circles are finished, work from the edge of the circles into the center. Follow each circle in turn, not concentrating on one alone, as it is easy to go too far and lose their symmetry. Once they start to meet, follow the shape into the center absolutely evenly.

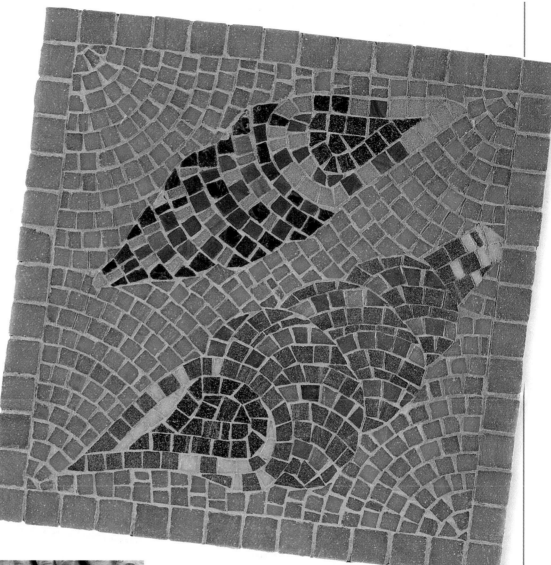

5 Once the mosaic is completely laid, fix by following the instructions for the indirect method.

▲ The Opus Circumactum is ideal for this panel because it gives the impression of waves or ripples, which complements the subject, as well as providing a lively—but not too distracting—background.

OPUS VERMICULATUM

Opus Vermiculatum describes the worm-like way mosaic tiles can flow round a form, creating a lively and interesting background. The tiles follow the contours of an image until they meet one another. The meeting point can be made in a sophisticated, seamlessly elegant way, or it can be a ragged, haphazard series of junctions. Both approaches have a certain appeal, and which one you choose probably depends on what the mosaic is for.

When people describe classical mosaics as having a sense of movement, this is very often the technique to which they are referring. Used on a large scale it can have a wonderful effect. You can use it to give a hierarchy to images by surrounding the most significant motifs with the widest following lines.

Opus Vermiculatum

YOU WILL NEED

Tools
Scissors
Board
Tile nippers
Adhesive brush
Grouting squeegee
Sponge
1/8in notched trowel

Materials
Brown paper
Permanent marker
Tiles
Water-soluble white craft glue
Grout
Cement-based adhesive

1 Cut a piece of brown paper slightly smaller than the board onto which you plan to fix your mosaic. Draw your design onto the matte side of the brown paper. It may be useful, as here, to sketch the lines of coursing onto the paper. Here, the movement of the fish's body is emphasized by being surrounded by flowing lines of tiles.

2 Lay the outer border tiles first, then the fish motif, sticking the tiles down with craft glue diluted 50:50 with water. You are then ready to lay the background. Follow the curving body of the fish. If this was a larger panel with more fish you would have lines of coursing around all of them, and you would have to make a decision about which lines were most important. There is no right way to treat these junctions. It is up to you to decide what arrangement you think looks most appealing.

3 Once the mosaic is complete, you will be able to see the full image in reverse. It is possible at this stage to make some minor adjustments to your tiles. Fix the mosaic by following the indirect method.

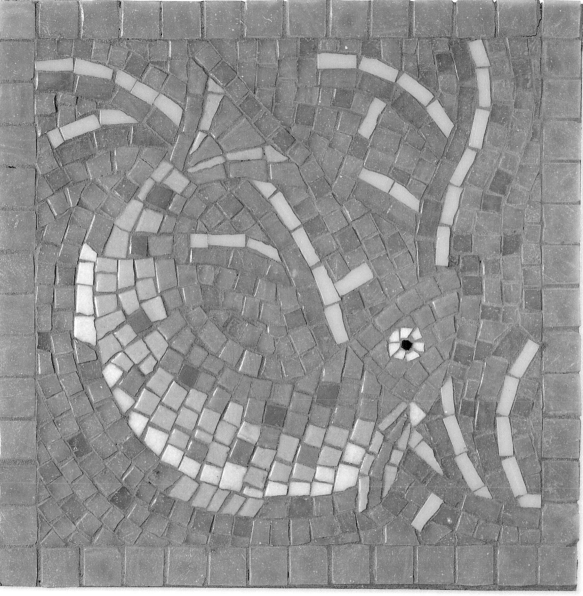

▲ Even within a small panel, Opus Vermiculatum gives a very dynamic effect.

Outdoor Direct Adhesive Method

Working with found materials, such as broken tiles, is a creative challenge. Although they are not all the same thickness, it is possible to build up the backs of the tiles with cement-based adhesive, thus producing a flat, practical surface.

A certain roughness is part of the appeal of broken-tile designs, which benefit from a free approach. The use of jagged tiles contributes to their distinctive charm. Although there is a general rule in mosaic making about not beginning with the background, in this case if the background contains the thickest tiles, that is where you must begin. Place a thin layer of adhesive under the thickest tile and a thicker layer under the thinner ones, but do not apply so much that the adhesive squeezes up between the joints. This project is a table intended for use outside. Make sure your adhesive is appropriate for exterior use.

YOU WILL NEED

Tools
Tile nippers
Spatula or small tool
Hammer
Small board
Knife for removing excess adhesive
Grouting squeegee
Lint-free cloth

Materials
Board cut from marine ply
Primer
Charcoal
Slow-setting cement-based
  exterior adhesive
Latex admix
Selection of tiles
Copper strip
Brass pins
Black grout

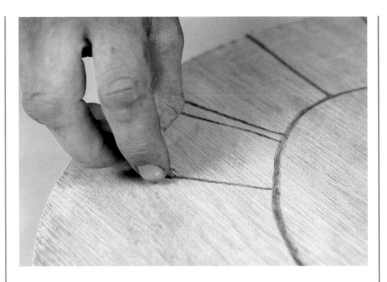

1 The base must be cut from marine ply, since other kinds of wood may not stand up to the elements. Prime the board. When the primer is dry, draw your design onto the board. Mix up some slow-setting cement-based adhesive. Some adhesives may require a latex admix to bond securely with wood. It is essential that the adhesive is slow-setting, because it will take time to lay all the tiles.

2 Begin by laying the area of your design that uses the thickest tiles. All the tiles need to be laid to the depth of the thickest tile in order to be perfectly flat, and by starting with the thickest tiles, you will establish a target height for all the other tiles. Apply adhesive with a spatula or small tool.

☞
**Direct method,
pages 74–77**

3 It is important to keep checking that the mosaic has been laid flat before the adhesive has set. To do this, you use a light hammer and a small board, gently tapping the area you have laid to ensure the surface is level. If the adhesive has already set, you risk breaking the bond. If adhesive squeezes up between the joints as you tap, scrape it away with a knife. If you find that some tiles are low, take them out and build up the level with more adhesive.

6 After the strip has been attached, grout the mosaic (see Grouting). A piece like this made by the direct method will only need to be grouted once. Clean the grout off with a sponge. Leave the tabletop to dry.

7 Once it has dried completely, buff the mosaic with a lint-free cloth. You can now attach it to your table base, using screws that will not rust.

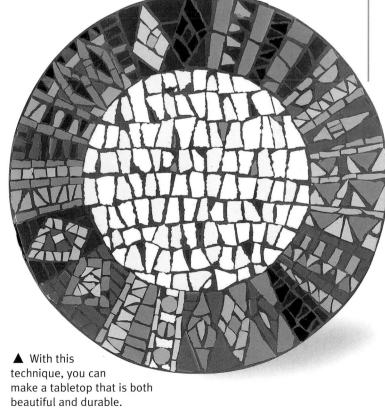

▲ With this technique, you can make a tabletop that is both beautiful and durable.

4 Once the thickest tiles have been laid, you can begin work on other areas. Again, the order of your work depends on the thickness of the tiles. In this design, the incorporation of a small number of brightly colored tiles enhances the liveliness of the gray and blue tiles.

5 When the mosaic is finished and the adhesive has set, pin a copper strip around the edge to protect it and to disguise the raw edges of the tiles. To prevent rust, use solid brass pins.

Outdoor Indirect Method

The indirect method is ideal for pieces that you plan to use outside. Using this technique, you can create your mosaic inside, without worrying about weather conditions. You can wait for a fine day to fix the mosaic.

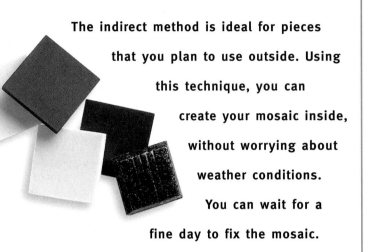

Make sure that the materials you are using are durable enough to be used externally. This applies not simply to the mosaic tiles, but also to the cement-based adhesive. Not all adhesives are frost-proof. Check the manufacturer's instructions to ensure that the adhesive you plan to use is suitable for the task.

YOU WILL NEED

Tools	Materials
Scissors	Board or surface to fix to
Tile nippers	Brown paper
Adhesive brush	Charcoal
Grouting squeegee	Water-soluble white craft glue
$\frac{1}{8}$in Notched trowel	Mosaic tiles, including unglazed ceramic and vitreous glass
Sponge	Grout
	Cement-based adhesive
	Latex admix

1 | Cut a piece of brown paper fractionally smaller than the ultimate size of your piece, and draw your design onto it. Prepare a 50:50 solution of craft glue and water.

2 | Use the brush to apply craft glue to small areas of the paper, not to the tiles. Begin fixing tiles to the most significant areas of the design.

☞

Indirect method, pages 92–95 Grouting, pages 88–91

3 | This design is based on cutting effects and makes creative use of the way the material fractures as it breaks. Once all the tiles have been applied, leave to dry.

4 | Pregrout the mosaic (see Grouting), making sure that all the gaps between the tiles have been filled.

6 | Trowel the adhesive onto the surface to which you wish to fix the mosaic, using the notches in the trowel as a gauge to achieve uniform depth. If the surface is vertical, the adhesive should be mixed thickly. Without folding it, pick up your mosaic, and place it into the adhesive. Press the surface firmly to ensure that it has made contact across all of the fixing bed.

7 | After wetting the paper with a moist sponge, leave it for five to ten minutes to absorb the moisture, rewetting if it seems to be drying out. When it has turned dark brown, peel from one corner toward the middle. If tiles start to come away, particularly at the vulnerable edges, you need to wet the paper again. If one or two tiles remain stuck to the paper, place them back by hand. Once the paper has been removed, sponge the grout smooth with a moist sponge, and leave to dry. Regrout and clean once it is dry to complete the mosaic.

5 | Wipe off excess grout with a moist sponge, using a single, flat, sweeping motion. Use a clean area of the sponge each time, or you are likely to reapply as much grout as you remove.

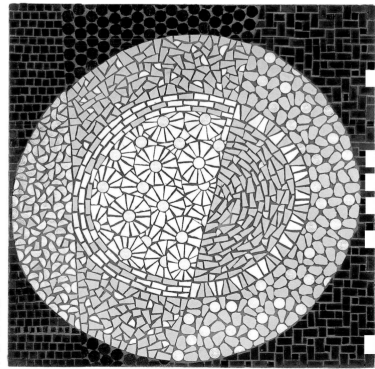

▶ This mosaic uses natural colors in unglazed ceramic, making it ideal for a feature panel in a Japanese-style garden.

Outdoor Sand and Cement

If you want to lay a flat exterior mosaic, but need to make it from materials that have a variety of thicknesses, you cannot use cement-based adhesive. The sand and cement method can greatly extend the range of what you can do outside.

By laying your tiles into a bed of sand and cement and then tapping a board over them before the cement sets, you can level out the surface and also ensure that all the tiles are securely held in place. This technique cannot be used in all locations, as the cement screed is thick and heavy. This is not a problem outside, which is where this method is extremely useful.

YOU WILL NEED

Tools	**Materials**
Carpenter's level	Sand
Rubber gloves	Cement
Trowel	Sheeted-up marble mosaic
Flat bed or grouting	on paper
squeegee	Grout
Hammer	Stone sealant
Board	
Sponge	

☞

Grouting, pages 88–91
Indirect method,
pages 92–95

1 To lay a sand and cement screed as a fixing bed, mix four parts sharp, washed sand to one part cement, then add water until you have a workable mixture. Lay the sand-cement mix in place, checking regularly with a carpenter's level to ensure a level surface. Depending on the position of the mosaic, you may need to lay some of your screed as a gentle slope to ensure that surface water runs off the mosaic. Once complete, leave the screed to dry (or cure) for at least a week.

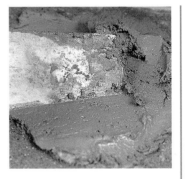

2 A cement slurry, a mixture of cement and water made to a creamy consistency, is used to fix the mosaic. Wet the cement screed and apply the slurry with a trowel, laying a thin but even quantity over the entire surface.

3 Pregrout the mosaic with cement slurry (see Grouting). Place it in position, then tap it all over using a board and a light hammer to ensure that the mosaic is in contact with the slurry, and that slight differences in thickness of the tiles are evened out by the bed below.

4 Wet the paper of the mosaic and leave to absorb the moisture for about ten minutes before peeling the paper off, drawing the paper gently back in a straight line. Wipe carefully with a moist sponge.

5 Once the mosaic is dry, regrout from the front.

6 Clean off thoroughly with a moist sponge. To give the mosaic resistance to staining, you can apply a special stone sealant.

▶ A thick and sturdy panel like this is ideal for the garden, or could be used for a path or feature for your front door.

Pebbles

Using pebbles instead of flat ceramic or glass tiles can give an interesting textural effect. The uneven surface which this method produces is not suitable for all locations, but it does work very well in the garden. These pebble slabs are good used as outdoor paving.

It is important to be sure that the materials you plan to use can withstand the weather conditions outside. You can mix different materials, but do not try to use domestic wall tiles, or any other materials which are not intended for exterior use, or the careful labor you put into making the mosaic will be wasted.

Always wear gloves when you work with cement, because it is very alkaline and can be bad for the skin.

YOU WILL NEED

Tools
Screwdriver
Rubber gloves
Wallpaper scraper
Flat bed trowel or
   squeegee
Plastic sheeting
Small decorator's brush
Spatula or small tool
Board
Hammer
Sponge

Materials
Casting frame (4 pieces of
   batten, 8 screws,
   backing board)
Petroleum jelly
Cement
Sand
Expanded metal lath (EML)
   or chicken wire
Selection of pebbles, tiles,
   terra-cotta tiles, and
   marble cubes

1 Spread petroleum jelly all over the inside of the casting frame (see Casting). Do not leave any gaps.

2 Mix together one part cement and three parts sand. Add water until it is firm and workable. Use the scraper to spread this in the frame to a depth of about one-third of your finished slab.

☞
Tesserae, pages 28–33
Casting, pages 58–61

3 Insert a sheet of expanded metal lath (EML) or chicken wire, slightly smaller than the size of the frame. This will give the slab strength. Cover the EML with the same amount of the sand and cement mix. Press flat with a flat bed trowel, or as here, a squeegee. Cover the wet slab with a sheet of plastic and leave to dry for a few days.

4 Once the sand and cement has had time to cure, you can apply tiles directly to it with a cement slurry. To make this, add cement to water until it has a thick creamy consistency. Remember to wear your gloves for these steps. Wet the slab, and spread the slurry onto it with the decorator's brush. With a small project, you can cover the whole area, but with larger projects you would only cover as much as you can manage quickly, perhaps one design element at a time.

5 Working quickly but carefully, inscribe the design into the slab with a spatula or small tool. Press the tiles firmly into the fixing bed. Here the design is simple, so it is advantageous to start with the border. If you worked from the center out, you might find at the end that you need to place small cut pieces on the vulnerable edge of the slab.

6 Once the border is in place, lay the central areas. The wide gaps caused by the irregularly shaped pebbles are a feature you can use to your advantage.

7 The finished surface may be uneven as tiles displace the cement slurry. You can solve this problem with a board and a hammer. Move the board across the mosaic, hammering gently as you go and continuing until you achieve an even surface. Take care removing the board: by beating the wet slurry up through the joints, you will have created enormous suction

between the board and the mosaic. Unless you break this pressure gently, by sliding the board off sideways, you'll lift tiles as you remove it.

8 Sponge the excess cement from the face of the mosaic, cover in plastic and leave to set for a couple of weeks. Once it is dry, remove the plastic, unscrew the frame, clean, and lay in position.

▼ Texture is the main feature of this small panel, as the white pebbles and their shadows stand out against the smoother black surface of the marble tiles.

Repeat Fan Patterns

You can work with repeating patterns in a structured or unstructured way, making them tesselate (fit together exactly) with one another, or you can repeat a pattern and use it as a decorative motif.

Making a pattern tesselate is complex. The fundamental principle behind successful repeat patterns is to minimize cutting and maximize planning, as is done here with this small tabletop. It is assembled using the indirect method and adorned with an interlocking fan design.

This is a relatively easy pattern to make tesselate, as it does not require too much complex cutting. Patterns which involve a series of diagonals, although they may look simple at first glance, are actually much trickier to produce in mosaic.

YOU WILL NEED

Tools
As for indirect method

Materials
Brown paper
Pair of compasses
Pencil
Permanent marker pen
Water-soluble white craft
  glue
Selection of tiles

☞
Borders, pages 56–57
Indirect method,
pages 92–95
Taking templates,
pages 122–125

1 This design is based on a series of tesselating fans. Fans are a geometric derivative of circles, created from the way they interlace. Draw a circle. Put the point of the compass on any point on the edge of the newly drawn circle and draw another. Where these two circles cross, place the point of the compass and draw another one. Continue until there are many interrelated shapes across the whole sheet of paper. If you look closely at the pattern you have just made, you will notice that the paper is covered with fan shapes. Select the orientation of the fans which you are going to use. There three obvious orientations: the fans could all be laid pointing to the right; they could all be laid pointing to the left; or they could alternate. This design takes the alternating option. Mark your choice on your sketch.

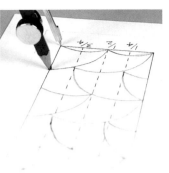

2 Decide how many repeats you want, based on the area you wish to cover and the size of the tile module. It is useful to produce a scaled-down drawing of your work at this point. Divide the design into four sections and draw guidelines from the top to the bottom. These guidelines give you a chance to check if the points of the fans line up accurately. It is surprisingly easy for little inaccuracies to occur, and small inaccuracies become much larger over a substantial area. Start from the bottom corner of the design.

3 This tabletop needs a border to give the design a sense of being contained. Sketch in a repeating border (see Borders for guidance). Color your drawing.

4 | Cut out a piece of brown paper to the size of the table top. Sketch in the guidelines you drew on your drawing. You can either draw every fan with a series of repeating circles using a compass, as in step 1, or, perhaps more neatly, you can create one fan to the size you require and make a template. You can then draw around this to create the entire design. The points of the fans should coincide with the guidelines.

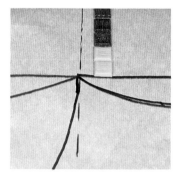

5 | The border is planned, taking into consideration the height and width of the tile module. A border that ended with a cut tile along one edge would look haphazard.

6 | Once the drawing is complete, you can cut your large piece of paper into smaller sections that are easier to work with. In this design the lines of division are based on the fan shapes. Once the paper is cut into pieces, you can begin sticking the tiles down.

7 | Although this design does not require a great deal of cutting, there are areas where the cutting is critical, especially along the edges of the fans. Cut the angled tiles first, then lay tiles into the center. You may have to trim central tiles to ensure an even fit. However, once the design is complete, you will not notice cut tiles in the center. If it is necessary to trim tiles for several lines in succession, make sure that the edges of cut tiles do not line up with one another.

▼ This design uses a random mix of colors, but you could emphasize the shapes by using gradated tones within each fan.

Taking Templates

The word "template" has two meanings. Sometimes it means a ready-made pattern, which can be useful for beginners who have not yet developed the confidence to create their own designs. In mosaics, the word has a special meaning. It refers to a paper, or sometimes board, form that represents the perimeter of an area you wish to cover in mosaic.

For example, if you wanted to make a mosaic for your bathroom, you would make a template of your bathroom floor, cutting around the sink stand and cutting out the area occupied by the bathtub or shower. Ultimately the template represents the size and shape of the work you have to produce to cover your bathroom floor in the most accurate way possible.

YOU WILL NEED

Tools
Ruler or yardstick
Pencil or pen
Permanent marker pen
Charcoal
Crayons

Materials
Layout paper
Brown paper
Tracing paper

☞
**Design techniques,
pages 70–73
Indirect method,
pages 92–95**

1 In the early stage, when you are first producing your design, you must have a good idea of the size of the area you wish to cover. Begin by producing a drawing to scale, basing your design on the colors you plan to use. It is helpful to draw the size of a single mosaic tile onto your scale drawing, to check that you are planning something realistic. Sometimes it is easy to allow your imagination to run wild, without taking into consideration how you will actually create the design you have planned.

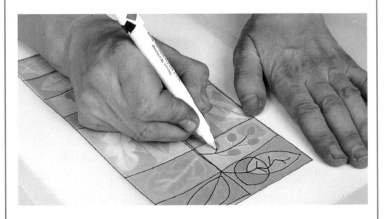

2 Once you have produced a design, draw it onto tracing paper, so you can reverse it later. Make sure you have included all the main features of your design.

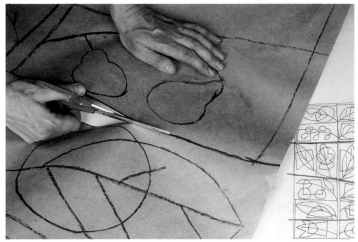

3 | This template, for a wall niche in a garden, was originally drawn onto sheets of newspaper. Mosaic cannot be made up on newspaper, so the newspaper template has to be transferred to a sheet of brown paper. This can be done either by measuring the newspaper and reproducing the dimensions, or simply by placing it on top of the brown paper and drawing around it.

It is easiest to make your templates on brown paper from the start whenever possible. Be sure you make the template on the matte side of the paper. Scribble over the back of the template to avoid possible confusion about which is the right side. It is also helpful to mark the top of the template.

5 | Once the design has been drawn on the paper, decide how you wish to divide up the mosaic into workable areas, keeping in mind what size area you like to work with and also the way in which the mosaic will finally be placed in position. As you can imagine,

very large sections can be heavy and unwieldy. Draw your section lines onto the tracing paper. Code the sections, marking this code on the original side of the tracing paper. This is now your key drawing or fixing diagram.

4 | Reproduce your reversed drawing on the matte side of the paper. If you drew it to scale in the first place, this task is easy, because you can simply scale off the original.

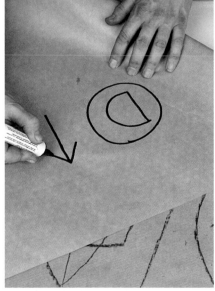

6 | Mark the section code onto the back of the template paper. Include directional arrows, because—and this is especially true of abstract designs— once the mosaic is covered with grout, it may not be obvious which way is up. Now you can begin to make the mosaic.

ENLARGING A DESIGN

A key part of the mosaic process is transferring your design from a nicely colored drawing that you have on a sheet of drawing paper into an accurate working template which shows you where to lay the tiles.

If you are very confident at drawing, this may not seem difficult. But if you are doing a complex design which has taken a long time to get right on paper, then you will want to be able to enlarge it accurately. The useful part of this process is that the grid you draw to help transfer your design can be the same grid as you use to divide up the whole mosaic into sections to be laid in the indirect method.

YOU WILL NEED
Tools
Ruler
Pencil
Charcoal

Materials
Tracing paper
Brown paper

1 Make a working drawing at a small scale and decide on the best way to divide it up into manageable sections. It is not normally sensible to have sections that will be much bigger than a couple of square feet if you are working in vitreous glass or

2 Having decided how many sections your design will be divided into, draw these sections up onto tracing paper.

☞
**Design techniques, pages 70–73
Indirect method, pages 92–95**

ceramic. If you are working in marble, which is a heavier material, the sections need to be smaller. These section lines will help as an aid to drawing your reversed design onto the brown paper.

3 Trace your design onto the tracing paper and number or letter the sections. You will use this as the key when you enlarge the design. The numbers will also remind you of the sequence of the sections and so help prevent them from being fixed out of order.

4 Once this has been done, draw the section lines onto the matte side of a piece of brown paper with a pencil. Write the key numbers or letters onto the back of the brown paper (the shiny side).

5 Turn over the tracing paper so that you are working in reverse. With the matte side of the brown paper uppermost, draw out the reversed design. The section lines give you assistance in reproducing the original accurately. Simply make sure that the enlarged design intersects your grid at the same positions as on the tracing paper grid. With this grid as guide, you will find the original surprisingly easy to recreate. If you need more detail you could subdivide the grid into halves or quarters.

WORKING AROUND A FIXED OBJECT

It is easy to be deceived about the shape of something. You may measure a space and find that it is one yard by two yards but, in reality, this doesn't tell you about all the swelling into the space of a wall, or the small area of molding around a fitted cupboard. These are just the sort of minor details that mean that your mosaic might not fit perfectly.

It is much easier to make a life-size template of an area, and be certain that your mosaic will slot exactly into place, than to spend the time trouble-shooting when it doesn't. You might well wish to take a template of a bathroom floor, as this is the sort of room where mosaic is very often used. In cases where it is not possible to move fixed pieces of sanitary ware, you will have to cut around them.

The whole area of a floor will not fit on a single piece of brown paper. The template will have to be constructed from a series of sheets of paper, stuck together on the shiny side with masking tape.

YOU WILL NEED

Tools
Scissors
Craft knife
Measuring tape
Ruler
Pencil

Materials
Tracing paper
Brown paper

☞
**Design techniques,
pages 70–73
Indirect method,
pages 92–95**

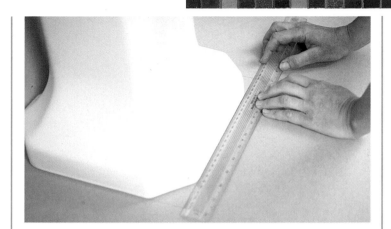

1 Some areas are easy to measure out with paper, particularly where there are no fixed objects. Where you do encounter an object, such as the pedestal of this basin, you will need to measure out its position and dimensions so you can mark them onto the brown paper.

2 The outer dimensions of the front and sides of this pedestal are easy to measure. The difficulty with any template comes with curves, which are less easy to measure precisely. The secret of making successful templates around curved areas is to be unafraid about cutting away too much paper. It is easy to patch paper back in around a curve. The angles at the corner of this pedestal were quite easy to measure but, had they not been, they could have been made by cutting out the general shape of the pedestal and then patching pieces of paper back in to fit the shape.

3 Once you have the outer dimensions of the object, draw them onto the brown paper. To draw angled sections of a template, measure from the corners of the general outline to the point where the object ends and transfer these measurements onto the brown paper. Then cut out the area where the object stands.

4 Place the brown paper in position in order to check the accuracy of your template. If the space left for the object is too small, cut more away with a craft knife. If the space is too big, make a patch so that it does fit precisely.

Three-dimensional Effects

Some of the very earliest mosaics used three-dimensionality to tremendous effect. The Roman portrait of a Campagnan woman, at the house of Julia Felix in Pompeii, is a fine example. The image is so fresh and life-like that you feel you could recognize her if you met her in person.

In order to create three-dimensional effects you have to use the tonal qualities of color. In the mosaic palette some colors are much better represented through a range of tones than others. It is easier to work in areas of the spectrum which have a good range of tones available. But tone alone is not enough. A sense of form needs to be created through the way the tiles are laid and how the grout lines flow, to accentuate the sense of three-dimensionality.

This section is a guide to some tips and some pitfalls you might encounter. One you have assembled your mosaic onto paper, use the indirect method to finish and fix it.

YOU WILL NEED
Tools
Adhesive brush
Tile nippers

Materials
Tracing paper
Colored pencils
Selection of vitreous
   glass tiles
Permanent marker
Brown paper
Water-soluble white
   craft glue

☞

Indirect method,
pages 92–95
Templates,
pages 122–125

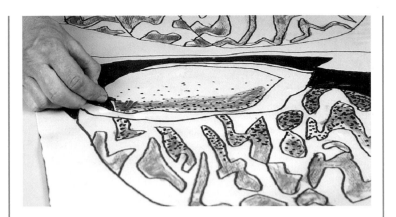

1 Produce a working drawing on tracing paper using colored pencils. To create a three-dimensional effect you need a subtle and gradual transition between tones. This does not mean you shouldn't use bright or intense colors, simply that your selection of colors should change gradually from shade to shade.

The sketch will be reversed and a complex design may need some clarification in the reversed sketch. Color in the main areas of the design so that you can distinguish them from the background.

2 Using a permanent marker, transfer the reversed design to the matte side of a sheet of brown paper (see Templates).

3 Before you glue the tiles to the paper, experiment in laying them in contrasting ways. Here, the tiles on the lower shell have been laid in straight lines across the design, producing a flat effect which is only accentuated by the grout. Follow the charcoal lines as a guide when you lay the tiles.

7 The impression of three-dimensionality is heightened by the contorted line which expresses the form of the shell and by the tonal variation of colors in the back- and foreground.

4 The tiles in the upper shell have been laid in a way which much better describes the form of the shell. They give a sense of the swelling shape the shell has. Once the tiles are positioned, it is possible to see how the shading and the lines of coursing of the tiles produce the sense of three-dimensionality.

6 The tonal gradation of bright colors for the shell gives a sense of three-dimensionality, while at the same time the straight-laid background has the opposite effect of flattening the piece.

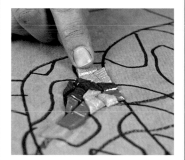

5 Lay the tiles, applying a little glue to the paper at a time. Remember to keep the tiles flowing along your guide-lines. Build the design up, working with a range of tones in both the brightly colored and the more muted areas.

▶ The shells motifs in this mosaic panel stand out in a clear and three-dimensional way from the background, because of the clever use of color.

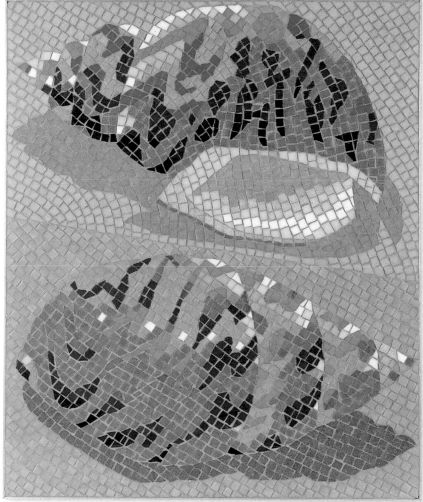

Three-Dimensional Surfaces

When tiles are laid in rows, the grout lines will naturally express a linear effect. However, three-dimensional objects, such as bowls, need special consideration, to find the best way to express the form through line.

If you stick with simple, economical cutting methods, the shape of the tiles does not detract from the intrinsic form of the object. In this bowl, rings of tiles follow the flaring shape, making the mosaic look as if it fits effortlessly. If you do not properly consider the form onto which you are laying tiles, it is suprisingly easy to lay them in a clumsy way. Plan how the lines will flow to avoid strange cuts or "seams", and draw your laying plan onto the surface before you start.

YOU WILL NEED

Tools
Paintbrush
Spatula or small tool
Grouting squeegee
Sponge

Materials
Primer
Slow setting cement-based
   adhesive
Latex admix
Vitreous glass mosaic tiles
Grout
Rubber gloves
Paint

☞
Direct method, pages
74–77
Common mistakes,
pages 64–65

1 Prime the bowl so that a cement-based adhesive will stick easily to its wooden surface. Once dry, make up some slow-setting cement-based adhesive. In this case, a latex admix has been combined with the adhesive in a 50:50 ratio with water, to give it extra grip onto wood. Ensure the adhesive mix is stiff: if it is too wet, the tiles may slip.

2 Apply adhesive to the bowl in small amounts, using the spatula. Use the adhesive mixture to flatten out the lip of the bowl, so that the first ring of tiles can be capped by a ring of tiles to finish neatly at the top.

3 | Follow the form of the bowl, laying the tiles directly into the adhesive in a series of rings. Always start from the top, so any problems with slippage will be immediately obvious. Be aware that adhesive is likely to squeeze up between the tiles in places where the angle of the bowl changes. On the flat base of the bowl, it is simpler to lay the tiles straight across, rather than cutting ever smaller angles into the center.

5 | Once the mosaic is dry, grout the bowl. Where the sides curve up, it is easier to grout by hand rather than with a squeegee, but make sure you wear rubber gloves. Sponge off any surplus grout.

6 | When the grout has dried, paint the outside of the bowl, and leave to dry.

4 | Reapply adhesive to the lip of the bowl, and lay the border tiles. Leave to dry for 24 hours.

▶ The laying of tiles on this bowl was carefully planned to give a seamless transition from the flat bottom to the curved sides.

Useful Tips

This section contains a few pertinent pieces of advice based on the experiences of mosaic-making. As soon you start working in the medium of mosaic you will soon develop tips of your own and find ways of working that suit you. You may even discover better techniques than the ones given here.

The fundamental principles—how you cut tiles, lay them in place, and fix them permanently into a mosaic—are covered in the other sections of this book. This section is intended more as a general look at the creative processes and some useful pointers to help you make successful mosaics. As you will see from all the methods shown in this A to Z of Techniques, the design and making processes are so intimately linked than you cannot separate them. That is part of the joy of making mosaics.

Above all: experiment. By trying out new ideas and not being frightened to have a few failures you are likely to create dramatic successes. What appear in this book as sets of rules and guidelines have in fact been aquired over the years through building up experience of different types of mosaic-making, and by being prepared to experiment to find ever-better techniques.

☞

**Design sources,
pages 14–18
Color in mosaics,
pages 18–25
Taking templates,
pages 122–125**

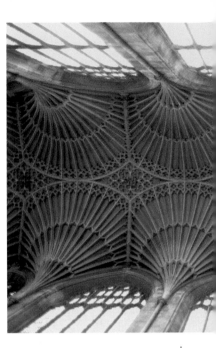

▲ Don't forget how useful it can be to produce a working drawing. If your design is complicated in terms of color or pattern it can be very helpful to work out potential problems on paper before you lay the mosaic. It is always quicker to produce and check a design on paper than it is to troubleshoot a half-completed mosaic.

▲ Don't always work from a drawing. This may seem to contradict the advice above, but in fact they goes hand in hand. It is easy to stifle your creativity in the act of translating your work from one medium to another. To produce effective designs you need to think about the way mosaic works best, and allow the medium to lead the way. Do not be restricted by the constraints a paper design can impose.

▲ Look around you. Mosaic is an immensely rich medium. It offers you the opportunity to think about a huge variety of visual effects and themes, such as color, tone, intensity, pattern, stylization, and the choice between matte and reflective surfaces. All of these are constantly on display in a vast experimental way in your everyday surroundings and places you might visit. Once you have become sensitive to what you see, you can draw inspiration from all sorts of phenomena you might not previously have observed.

▲ Research. If you are finding one area of work in mosaic difficult—tone perhaps, or color—it can help to study pieces which you think use these effects well. Some mosaicists keep a library of mosaic images. Once your friends know you are interested in mosaic you will undoubtedly receive lots of mosaic postcards. Don't think you can derive inspiration only from images of mosaic though. It can be helpful to collect any kind of picture you find interesting or inspiring. You might find particular color combinations, or shapes, or ways of composing an image, useful as reference material. Printed material can show how to derive a huge number of effects and approaches from a limited palette of colors. Don't be afraid to imitate effects from other media.

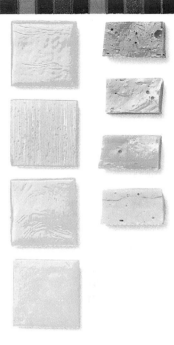

◀ Mix media. In order to explain how some of the techniques in this book work, and what the effects given by the various materials are, the projects have tended not to mix media very much. This is not intended as a guide to how you should work. Combining materials can be an exciting way of extending the color and surface qualities of any range. When working direct, as in Katie Hall's panel shown here, you can combine almost any materials. You can also mix media when working indirect, as long as the materials are all of approximately the same thickness.

▲ Keep an eye on color. Remember that there is often a variation between different batches of the same color tiles from a different or even the same supplier. If you are working on a large mosaic with one primary background color, make sure you have enough material before embarking on the mosaic. It can be very frustrating, and look rather strange, if the background color changes slightly halfway across a piece. If this does happen, however, it can be remedied. Rather than soaking off all the mosaic and starting again, randomly peel off some tiles in the area you have already laid, and make a mixture of the old and the new color batches across the whole area, to give an interesting and flickery effect.

GALLERY

Gallery

This section is intended to inspire you by

showing finished mosaics of various

subjects made in

different styles.

They are arranged in

themes, such as andamenti,

color, or relief, so that you can

start to analyze what makes each

one special. Once you start

making mosaics, you will quickly

develop your own style and will

be able to apply that style to

fresh ideas of your own.

ANDAMENTI
Andamenti are the ways in which the grout lines course through a mosaic. Subtle variations in the way these are done can animate and give a feeling of energy to a mosaic. Andamenti work most effectively if the spacing between tiles is absolutely even and regular throughout. Jerky and uneven spacing can interfere with the sense of rhythm that is created by the joints between tiles and the flow of grout lines.

▼ This is a mosaic depicting hoopoes. The inspiration for it came from Indian miniatures, the colors of which are wonderfully rich and subtle. The mosaic is made from marble, terra-cotta, and silver leaf. The background has been laid in rather a static way that gives emphasis to the more interesting feathery patterns used on the bodies of the birds. Note how on the left of the piece, the andamenti begin to express movement, suggesting shimmering heat.

► This mosaic was made using unglazed ceramic. The design is intended to suggest its source of inspiration, which was the color, pattern and themes used on Indian rugs. The grout lines are coursed in order to maximize the effect of the cut tiles and minimize the amount of cutting needed.

▲ Here, the coursing of grout lines assists in the description of form. The variety of directions in which the tiles are laid, and the layering effect of using one method of coursing on top of another, helps to give a sense of depth and complexity, further aided by the richness of the colors used.

COLOR

One of the real excitements of working in mosaic is the fact that you have to learn how to use color in a striking and readable way. The limitations imposed by having to work with a fixed palette force you to concentrate on your choices of color. Once you have built up your confidence, you will be amazed by the breadth of color treatments you can achieve in mosaic.

► This is a detail from the mosaic of an underwater scene shown opposite. Here, the color of the fish contrast stongly with the color of the water. The weed is laid in a dynamic way, giving movement to the scene. The darker tones used in the weed bring the lighter ones forward and give an impression of depth.

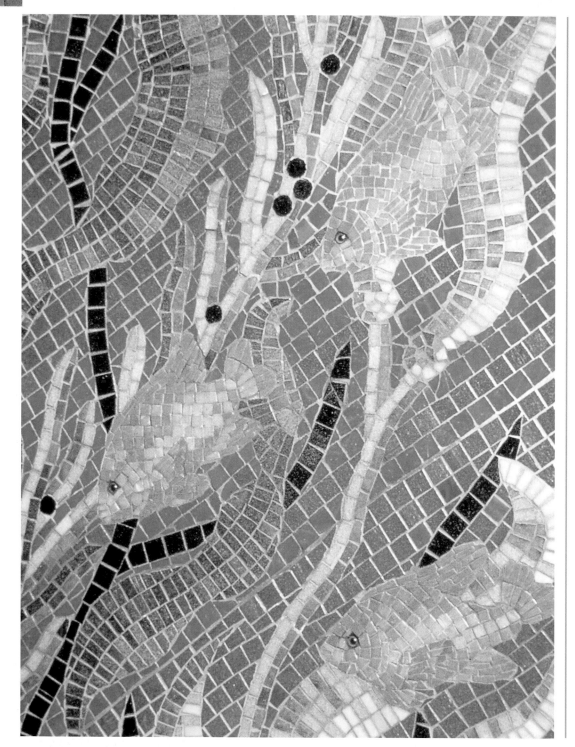

◀ This lively mosaic was made from vitreous glass tiles. The fishes' bodies are described by subtle tonal transitions. Slight differences in the angles at which we view them help to animate the group. Note the different kinds of cuts that are used in this piece.

▼ The break in background color in this section has been made carefully. The eel, as it wriggles down through the water, helps to draw the eye to the depths. The clown fish delicately straddle the line where the color changes, and it is only as you look closely that your eyes are drawn further down by the half-hidden tones of the catfish.

◀ These mirrors both demonstrate effective and interesting ways in which color can be used. The circular mirror is an exercise in subtle tonal color within the leaves. The grapes contrast effectively with their background. The oval mirror divides the shape into sections in order to try out various combinations of color, contrast, and intensity.

CUTTING

You can achieve a whole range of effects by varying the ways in which you cut the tiles. The most traditional method of cutting tiles is to shape them into small squares, but there are other ways of cutting which can be interesting and effective. There are many examples of traditionally cut mosaics shown throughout the gallery chapter of this book. This section demonstrates how well other approaches to cutting can work.

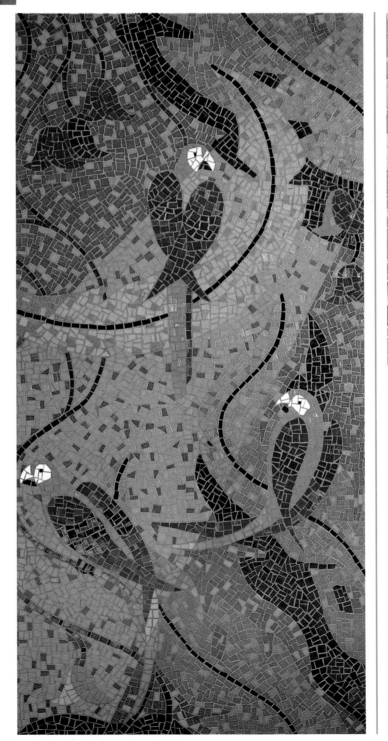

► These parrots are made with vitreous glass tiles. The curving movement of their bodies is picked up by the curves of the large tropical leaves. The shaft of light in the center of the mosaic uses a simple contrast of colors, predominantly light blue-green with dots of dark blue-green. In the shady areas this scheme is reversed, giving harmony to the whole piece.

▲ This detail from a large mosaic made with vitreous glass tiles demonstrates how you can give emphasis to an object with contrasting cutting treatments. The circular-shaped seeds contrast with the linear treatment of the pods, and the different cutting methods heighten the impact of the circles.

► These haphazard cuts work well to give a scaly effect to this marine scene. This way of cutting has worked well in this mosaic because it has helped to give an impression of the fractured, rippling light effects you can sometimes see on the surface of water.

▼ This tabletop demonstrates the subtlety of the Opus Palladianum method. The petals of the sunflower are strikingly veined, while the center of the flower gives an impression of depth because the grout is close in tone to the color of the tiles. Fractured cuts are appropriate to the organic form of the flower.

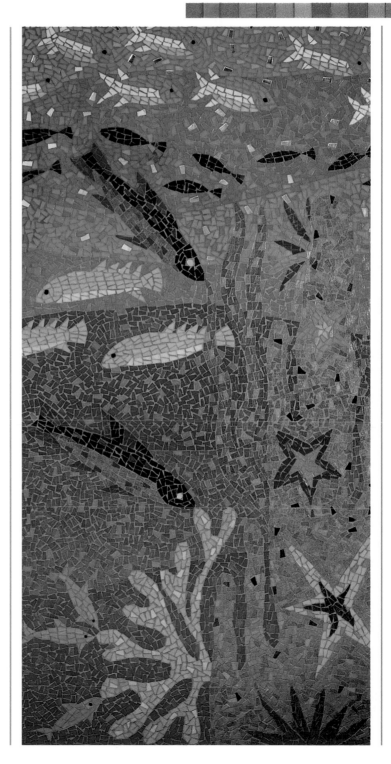

CONTRAST

Readability (how clearly you can see the images) can be a problem in mosaic. Grout can turn what might have seemed like a clear image while you were laying the tiles, into something rather difficult to distinguish. The best way to avoid this problem is to choose colors with high contrast. Although all the pieces in this section are in color, black and white tiles can also be used to great effect, as the contrast between them gives power and clarity to any image.

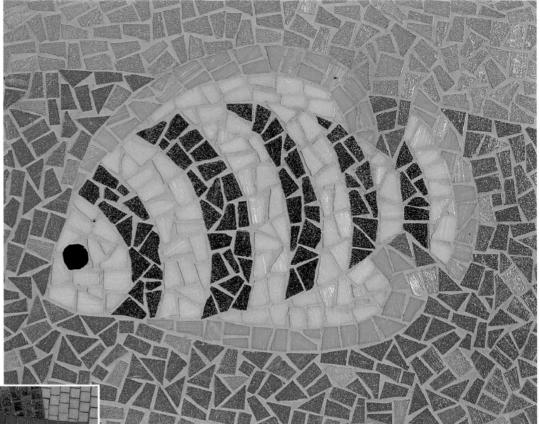

▲ The subject matter of this mosaic is immediately identifiable. If the mosaic had been made in a mid to dark acqua-green, this would not have been the case. The reason for the clarity is the intense color contrast. On some occasions clarity is more important than others. Lettering would be a good example of when it is useful to make your image as contrasting as possible.

◄ If the contents of this bowl had not been surrounded by the lighter color of the bowl itself, the image would have been very unclear, as the tone of the contents and the tone of the tablecloth is very similar. It is the bright contrast of the bowl which makes the image comprehensible.

▲ Tonal and color contrasts make this image readable. It is not sufficient, though, that colors contrast in hue. They also have to work well with one another, as the colors of these fruit do. Note that this mosaic is largely made with uncut tiles, and still works well.

LIGHT EFFECTS

Light effects is a phrase which can describe a variety of things. It can mean the way in which mosaic is arranged to catch the light, or it can refer to the way light is depicted. Some of the mosaics in this section employ the properties of reflected light as part of the design. Light and shade can also be used to give a sense of form to an object.

▼ This jewelry box by Fran Soler was inspired by Byzantine mosaics. It uses an unusual technique to catch the light. A plain wooden box was first coated with gold shiny paper and then mosaiced with glass and colored tiles. The effect is dazzling but the piece was quite affordable to make.

▲ This mosaic uses light to give a sense of form to its culinary theme. Look at the way the paella pan is highlighted around the rim, and the shading from one side of the pan to the other. The shape of the langoustines is brought to life through the use of tonal color transitions.

► These mosaics were made for the dining room of a cruise liner. The stars are picked out by gold and silver tesserae, and the lines which describe the imaginary forms of the constellations vary in tone, which helps to give them a shimmering quality.

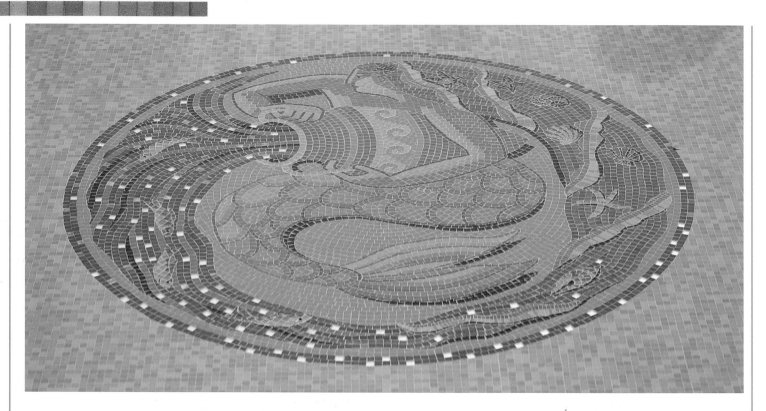

▲ This mosaic of Aquarius in the form of a mermaid is made in vitreous glass. The bold, graphic design is linked with its watery surroundings by using tiny pieces of mirror scattered throughout the background. These tiles, seen as bright dots in this photograph, change the appearance of the mosaic according to the brightness of the light from day to day.

◄ This mosaic for a patio uses mirror glass in a similar way to the one above. It is an aerial view of the client's house and surrounding area. It is largely made in ceramic, with tiny dots of intensely colored glass used to represent cars on the roads surrounding the house.

PATTERN

Pattern is in the nature of mosaic. Any design which is made up through a series of minute pieces must have pattern as one of its essential elements. It is easy to sideline the effects of pattern, but if you play on what the material does naturally it is easy to produce exciting results.

▶ Wendy Davison's sun panel uses a slightly irregular pattern of sunrays to bring motion to what could otherwise have been a rather static image. The strong color contrasts between the red outline of the rays and the blues and yellows of the sun and background help to convey an impression of heat.

◀ This mosaic, made in vitreous glass, uses the reverse face of the mosaic for its textural qualities. Repeated forms and repeated shapes are treated with minute differences. It is these little variations which really bring the patterns to life.

▲ Marble and terra-cotta have been used here for an entrance floor to a hotel. The design depicts the patterns shown on a nautilus shell. The minute, but structured, differences of tone and color make the pattern lively. Notice how well a single pattern can work over a large area.

◄ This marble tabletop shows a series of moths. The interest of the design is in the limited use of colors, and the complexity of the camouflage patterns on the moths' wings.

▼ The semi-abstract nature of this underwater landscape uses pattern in a sophisticated and complex way. Some sections have quite formal patterns, such as the overlapping wave effect at bottom right. Other areas have apparently random lines within them. Note how changes of direction in the andamenti help to convey the effect of seaweed rising between beds of coral.

▲ Ceramic has been used for this mosaic at the entrance of a house. The design is divided into two halves, land and water, with the background patterns suggesting the nature of the two. Look at how the tones of the tiles have been used to help distinguish one pattern from the next. It is also a good example of how details and different images can be set within a strong pattern.

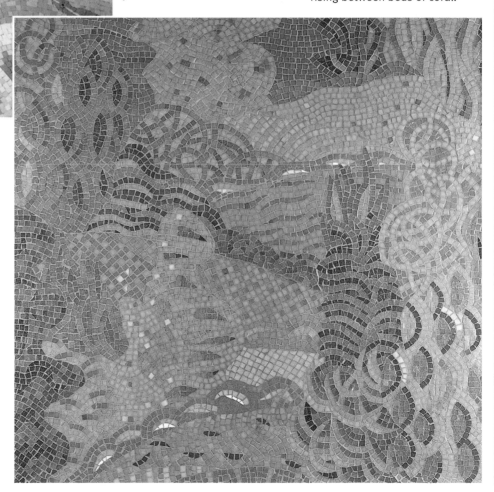

REALISM

This term encompasses quite a range of approaches to mosaic. It could refer to the intense, painterly realism of micromosaic, but it is also sometimes used simply to refer to the depiction of objects from the real world. Whether you are interested in stylized objects or near-photographic accuracy, it is possible to create the effect you want in mosaic.

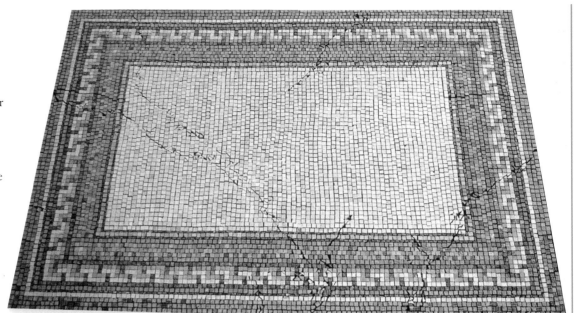

▲ This mosaic reproduces another kind of realism, that of age. It was carefully constructed for a client's shower-room floor, to look like a mosaic which had withstood the ravages of time. The "cracks" were all carefully cut and made to look as authentic as possible.

◀ These apples hanging from a string were derived from a Spanish still-life painting. The background is cast into deep shadow behind the apples, and the effect is particularly realistic because of the sharp shadows cast by the strings. The apples are given a vivid sense of form by the way that the lines of tiles curve around their shapes.

◄ This shower-room was made for a client who also used his adjacent library as a guest-room. He liked the idea of having the shower continue the theme, so the whole shower-room was lined with mosaic books.

RELIEF

One of the charms of mosaic is its range. You can have used all the different materials, experimented with every color, cut the tiles and laid them in every permutation you can think of, and still not have exhausted what it has to offer. One vast area, which offers a new way of viewing all these elements, is to work with relief, texture, or three-dimensional form. When you are creating an image which employs these properties you have to consider light and shade as part of the design.

▼ This mosaic of Gemini is made in smalti. The highly reflective enamelled glass has a faceted face and is very reflective of light. This is the kind of glass that was used in Byzantine churches. The movement expressed by the floating figures works well in contrast to the static background.

◀ This witty mosaic by Vanessa Benson shows kebabs on sticks. Some marble really does look very meaty and Vanessa, noticing this, has made a very effective bas-relief from it. She has used marble and smalti on a plain marble field, which is effective as it does not interfere with the readability of the image.

▶ This entertaining mosaic of a dog by Stewart Hale is made from glazed ceramic tiles. The multitude of joints in mosaic make it easy to work around a three-dimensional form. This piece uses the tiles in a freely fractured way, but it is also possible to use them in a more structured fashion.

▶ Working around a three-dimensional form can present quite a challenge to a mosaicist. For these candlesticks Steve Wright and Donald Jones have chosen to emphasize the fractured nature of the process by using completely random tiles of broken crockery.

▼ Here Tim Coppard has used pebbles in an almost lace-like way. He is interested in the minute differences between surfaces, which he has thrown into higher relief by laying them in a similar manner. This gives the mosaic a very pleasing rhythm.

▼ This lively mosaic is an assemblage by Norma Vondee. Note how she has used color contrast and reflective surfaces to give readability to a busy piece. Contrasting sizes of tile also vary the impression given by the background.

▲ Mirror frames are always a good starting point for small experiments with different kinds of techniques. They are small enough to allow you to experiment freely without spending too much time or money. This mirror was an experiment with how a textural surface would contrast with a reflective surface.

TONE

Tone, like contrast can be an aspect of color. It is an important element to master as it can make all the difference as to whether or not an image is readable. Grout of different tones can fuse the tile tones together or fracture them entirely. Natural materials such as marble may have tonal variation within a single piece, and you can often get exciting results by using this natural variation.

▶ This mosaic shows the way in which the tone of the gray grout unites the mid-tones of the watery background. The gray also fractures the black and white birds evenly, but is most effective on the duck in the middle, whose gray colors are given greater clarity by the unifying effect of similarly-toned grout.

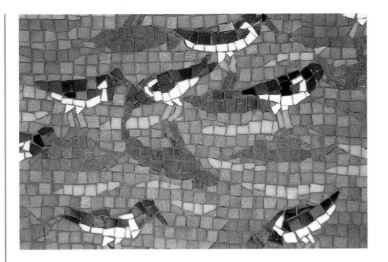

◄ This is a tiny mosaic of oystercatchers feeding in mud. The close tones of the background and the broken rhythm of the tiles give a watery feeling of reflective light to the piece.

▼ This tabletop uses the flickery tonal variation of the marble and demonstrates the way different colors have a tendency to fuse together if they are tonally close. Look at the red and brown marble around the edge of the tabletop. This tendency of close tones to merge together can be a virtue, or in some cases, a problem.

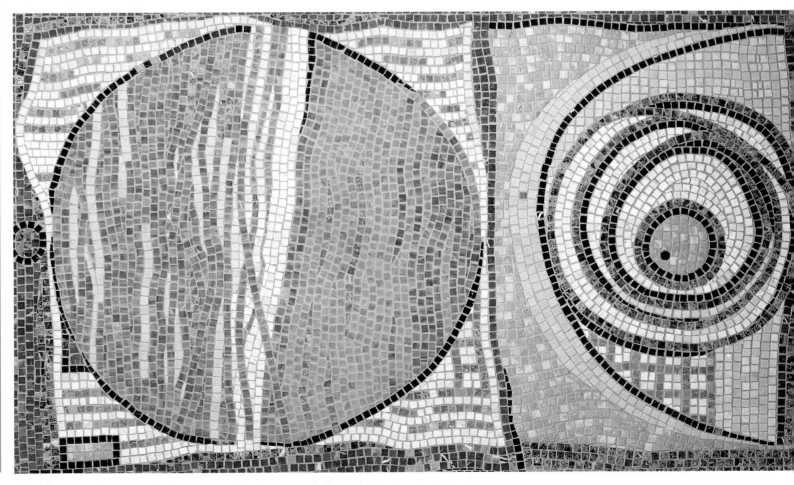

Glossary

ANDAMENTI
These are the lines along which mosaic tiles are laid, the lines of coursing of the mosaic.

BUTTERING
To butter the back of mosaic tiles is to coat the reverse face with a layer of adhesive or cement slurry.

CASTING
The process of making a solid mosaic object, such as a sand and cement slab within a mold.

CASTING FRAME
The frame or mold within which a slab is made and set.

CEMENT
A mixture of calcinated limestone and clay which, when mixed with sand and water, can be used as a base or backing for a mosaic piece.

CEMENT SLURRY
Cement mixed with water to form a creamy mixture which can be used to grout mosaic tiles.

COURSING
The coursing of tiles is like the coursing of bricks in a building. It is a term which describes the lines along which the tiles are laid, and can refer to the way they line through with one another.

CURING
To cure is to leave cement to set. Curing time is the time it takes for a cementitious mixture to set solid. Curing is also sometimes referred to as "going off."

CUTTERS
A hinged cutting tool for mosaic.

DIRECT METHOD
The method by which mosaic is laid directly in its permanent location, straight onto its final surface.

EMBLEMA
This term describes a highly sophisticated, finely made mosaic panel used as the center piece of a floor. Roman emblema were often made so that they could be moved from one location to another.

FEATHERING
Building up the depth of adhesive or sand and cement gradually to bridge a transition between levels on an uneven surface.

FIXING
To fix a mosaic is to set it in its final location. The fixing process is the process of setting it in place if it has been laid out in the indirect method. If working in the direct method the laying and fixing process are done at the same time.

GROUT
The cementitious matrix which fills the gaps between tiles. Grouting refers to the process of applying grout to a mosaic.

HONED MARBLE
Marble which has been polished to a matte rather than a glassy finish.

INDIRECT METHOD
A technique whereby mosaic is stuck in reverse onto a temporary surface before being turned over and fixed into place.

LAYING
To lay is to put the individual tiles of a mosaic in place.

MICROMOSAIC
Micromosaic is mosaic made from very tiny cut tiles. These can also be used within an ordinary mosaic but to qualify for the term micromosaic the whole piece must be executed with minute tesserae.

OPUS
This is the Latin word for work.

PREGROUTING
To pregrout is to grout a mosaic made by the indirect method from the reverse face before it is fixed in place.

RENDER
Sand and cement on a wall used as a substrate onto which to fix mosaic.

RIVEN MARBLE
Marble which has been cut in order to reveal its crystalline inner face.

SCREED
A sand and cement sub-base on a floor onto which mosaic can be fixed.

SETTING
This term is used both to describe the process of curing cement, and also to describe placing something in position.

SMALTI
Enamelled glass of the kind used in Byzantine mosaics.

TESSERAE
These are the components of a mosaic, which may include cut and uncut tiles, pebbles and found objects.

UNGLAZED CERAMIC
Ceramic tiles which have not been glazed with color. They are the same color throughout, rather than having just a surface color as with common household tiles.

VITREOUS GLASS
Square mosaic tiles made in molds from glass paste. They have a smooth top surface and a rough back.

Index

(SSD) in parentheses following a page number refers to a step-by-step demonstration in the A to Z of Techniques.

Credits

Quarto Publishing would like to thank and acknowledge
the following for photographs reproduced in this book:

e. t. archive: p. 10, p. 11 t+b, p. 12.
Clark/Clinch: p. 13 b
Wendy Davison: p. 145 t
Vanessa Benson: p. 151 t
Stewart Hale: p. 151 b
Tim Coppard: p. 152 l
Norma Vondee: p. 153 r

key: t = top b = bottom
     l = left r = right

All other images of finished mosaics in the Gallery section
appear courtesy of Emma Biggs and the Mosaic Workshop.

All other photographs are the copyright of
Quarto Publishing plc.